18 5-0

DANCE WITH YOUR SOUL

Jean Callander Milligan

DANCE WITH YOUR SOUL

A Biography of

JEAN CALLANDER MILLIGAN, LL.D.

Co-founder of The Royal Scottish Country Dance Society

by

Alastair MacFadyen, M.A., Ph.D., Dip.Ed.

RSCDS Glasgow Branch Chairman
RSCDS Hon. Archivist and RSCDS Vice-Chairman

and

Florence H. Adams

RSCDS Glasgow Branch President
RSCDS Chairman 1964–1967

© Royal Scottish Country Dance Society
First Published 1983
ISBN 0 902997 02 5

Printed by Clark Constable (1982) Ltd., Edinburgh

Contents

Foreword

By the RT. HON. THE EARL OF MANSFIELD, D.L., J.P.
President of the Royal Scottish Country Dance Society

Those of us who are privileged to be Scots will know of the great influence which Scottish Country Dancing has had in many parts of the world and which has cemented relationships of thousands of people of Scottish descent with the country of their forebears. Not so many will know of the Royal Scottish Country Dance Society and in particular of its co-founder, Dr Jean Milligan.

This courageous woman devoted her life to the preservation and revival of Country Dancing and the accompanying tunes. When she and Mrs Stewart of Fasnacloich founded the Society in 1923, traditional dancing in Scotland had sunk to a low ebb, and it was in some danger of extinction. By the time of her death in 1978 membership of the Society had spread throughout the world and with 120 Branches and over 300 Affiliated Groups, Scottish Country Dancing had not only been preserved but was flourishing as never before. People from many diverse races who had little in common with Scotland and yet had come to love and appreciate its music and dancing discovered a new and exciting bond.

Dr Milligan is shown in this book as one of that rare breed of person, that is to say a woman with a vision and with the ability and tenacity to grasp it and make it become reality. And yet as this book brings out, here was no stern teacher but a woman of immense zest for life, full of joy and gaiety and with a great love of her fellow human beings. But above all Scottish Country Dancing is fun for all those who take part – so let all those who derive so much enjoyment from it spare a thought once in a while for her who did so much to preserve and enhance it.

Mansfield

Authors' Note

When we were asked to prepare a biography of Jean Callander Milligan, we embarked on the assignment with some apprehension, realising that the biographers' task is not an easy one, particularly when their subject is the co-founder of The Royal Scottish Country Dance Society. We were fully aware of the difficulty of attempting to convey to the reader, a personality so dynamic and so diverse as that of Dr. Jean Milligan and of trying to capture between the covers of a book, a life so rich in endeavour and achievement.

Any success we may have had in presenting Dr. Milligan as a person is due almost entirely to those among her family, close friends and acquaintances who responded so willingly and generously to our request for their reminiscences. We hope that those who helped us with their memories will recognise in our work the "great lady" whom they knew and that those who did not have the privilege of knowing her may, on reading this biography, appreciate the feeling of one correspondent, who said, "She was, and is, unique."

We owe a great debt of gratitude to many people. In addition to those from near and far who answered our appeal for help, we received invaluable and much appreciated assistance from the staffs we consulted in libraries and archives, and in the Colleges and organisations with which Dr. Milligan was associated. All whom we met during our preparation of the biography, even those not directly linked with Dr. Milligan and Scottish country dancing, were genuinely interested in the purpose of our enquiries and gave generously of their time and expertise. We are especially indebted to Miss Isobel Elliot, Glasgow, who read our first draft with patience and care and offered helpful suggestions for improvement.

Alastair MacFadyen
Florence H. Adams
Glasgow, May 1983

Abbreviations

SCDS   The Scottish Country Dance Society
RSCDS   The Royal Scottish Country Dance Society

A view of Hillhead from Glasgow University Tower, 1905. Wellington Church is in the foreground and Bothwell Terrace (Bank Street), Jean Milligan's birthplace and family home, is half way up the picture on the right hand side. (Picture by courtesy of the Mitchell Library, Glasgow)

Family and Childhood

When the residents of the burgh of Hillhead opened their *Glasgow Herald*s on Saturday, 10th July 1886, there were several items of news which would be of interest to them. On the international front, they would note that Prince Otto von Bismarck, Imperial Chancellor of Germany, was planning to confer soon in Vienna with his counterparts of the Russian and Austrian empires. Of more immediate interest were the results of the General Election of the previous day. The new Member of Parliament for the Partick Division, of which Hillhead was a part, was the Unionist Liberal, Mr. Alexander Craig Sellar, the son of Mr. Patrick Sellar who earlier in the century had been responsible for the notorious Strathnaver clearances in Sutherland. If the *Herald* readers had their minds on the forthcoming Fair holiday, they would see that they could enjoy a sail to Inveraray and back on the paddle steamer "Lord of the Isles" for the price of a single ticket at 3s. 6d.[1] No doubt many of the readers would also note with interest the following item of very local news:

> MILLIGAN – at 7 Bothwell Terrace, Hillhead, on 9th inst., the wife of James Milligan; a daughter.

Thus in this very simple announcement was recorded the birth of Jean Callander Milligan. Apart from the years 1950 to 1954 when she and her sisters took up residence in the Lanarkshire village of Coulter, Jean Milligan lived all her days in the west end of her beloved city of Glasgow, never very far distant from the place of her birth.

Milligan Family Tree

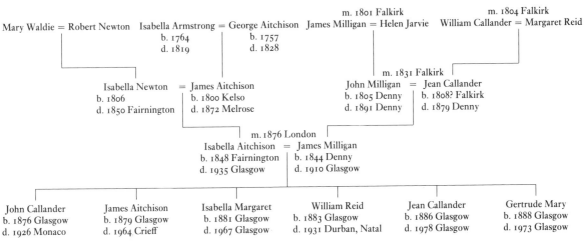

m. 1801 Falkirk

Mary Waldie = Robert Newton   Isabella Armstrong = George Aitchison   James Milligan = Helen Jarvie
b. 1764   b. 1757
d. 1819   d. 1828

m. 1804 Falkirk

William Callander = Margaret Reid

Isabella Newton   = James Aitchison
b. 1806   b. 1800 Kelso
d. 1850 Fairnington   d. 1872 Melrose

m. 1831 Falkirk

John Milligan   =   Jean Callander
b. 1805 Denny   b. 1808? Falkirk
d. 1891 Denny   d. 1879 Denny

m. 1876 London

Isabella Aitchison   =   James Milligan
b. 1848 Fairnington   b. 1844 Denny
d. 1935 Glasgow   d. 1910 Glasgow

John Callander   James Aitchison   Isabella Margaret   William Reid   Jean Callander   Gertrude Mary
b. 1876 Glasgow   b. 1879 Glasgow   b. 1881 Glasgow   b. 1883 Glasgow   b. 1886 Glasgow   b. 1888 Glasgow
d. 1926 Monaco   d. 1964 Crieff   d. 1967 Glasgow   d. 1931 Durban, Natal   d. 1978 Glasgow   d. 1973 Glasgow

James Milligan, father of the baby girl, was already in 1886 a well known and much respected figure in the city of Glasgow. A native of Denny in Stirlingshire where his father was a tailor, James Milligan had achieved notable success in the teaching profession.[2] He began his teaching career as a pupil teacher in Falkirk Parish School, and this was followed by two years of training at the Established Church Training College, Dundas Vale, Glasgow. The College Registers show that he was awarded a first class certificate at the end of his first year and a second class in 1865, his final year.[3] His first teaching appointment was in St. Andrew's Parish School, Glasgow, and in August 1866 he was appointed to the headship of Mitchell School, which was maintained in Piccadilly St., Anderston, by Wellington Street United Presbyterian Church. In charge of the younger scholars at the school was Miss Margaret Milligan, James' eldest sister. It is interesting to note that when Wellington Street Church decided to discontinue the school, brother and sister proposed to continue it themselves for two years, by which time it was hoped that the newly formed School Board of Glasgow would assume responsibility for it. Their proposal was accepted and the Church Session offered them an annual grant of £50 and the schoolroom free of rent.[4]

Whilst holding teaching appointments in Glasgow, James Milligan attended University classes and obtained the degree of Master of Arts. His scholastic and administrative abilities were recognised by the School Board of Glasgow when he was made head in 1878 of a newly opened school in Garnethill where he was to achieve his most outstanding success. Under his leadership the school quickly established a reputation for academic excellence, particularly among the girl pupils who won places at London and Cambridge Universities at a time when Glasgow University still refused them admission. It was James Milligan's concern and enthusiasm for the education of girls which eventually persuaded the School Board to raise Garnethill School to the status of a "higher-class" school for girls under the name of the Glasgow High School for Girls. He continued as the school's headmaster until 1905 when he retired due to ill-health. His distinguished career in Scottish education was acknowledged in 1901 when Glasgow University, on the occasion of its Ninth Jubilee, conferred upon him the honorary degree of Doctor of Laws.[5] When Dr. Milligan died in 1910 the following obituary appeared in the *Glasgow Herald*:

> In many respects Dr. Milligan was an ideal teacher. To a shrewd knowledge of character he added the faculty of being able to bring to bear on the pupils the influence of the well trained minds of a capable staff, and of arousing in them some of his own quality of indomitable perseverance and enthusiasm for learning.[6]

The Milligan children had the opportunity to benefit from their father's educational ideas because they all attended his school, the three boys for as long as it was a mixed public school and the three girls for their entire schooling. Before transferring to Garnethill, the boys were pupils at Glasgow Academy; William, the youngest son, returned there to complete his school career. Three of the family obtained University degrees. James, the second son, finished his schooling at Trinity College, Glenalmond, Perthshire, and graduated from Glasgow University with an honours degree in Classics. A year at Brasenose College, Oxford, resulted in successful admission to the Indian Civil Service, in which he spent the rest of his working life. The daughters, Margaret and Gertrude, were also graduates of Glasgow University; Margaret obtained a first class honours degree in English and Gertrude a second class honours degree in Classics. In 1915 Margaret was appointed to the staff of Dundas Vale Training College

The Milligan Family ca.1900. Standing (left to right): John, James, William. Seated (left to right): Jean, Dr. Milligan, Mrs. Milligan, Margaret. Seated in front: Gertrude.

and in 1923 was transferred from the College to Jordanhill College School, where she remained as Principal Teacher of English until her retirement in 1941. Gertrude Milligan was a teacher of Classics and spent the last eighteen years of her career on the staff of Hillhead High School, Glasgow. When she retired in 1948, the school magazine noted, in addition to her fine qualities as a teacher, that Miss Milligan's "youthful spirit found vent in country dancing and on the badminton court, where she combined dexterity with lightness of foot."[7]

As pupils at their father's school, the Milligan children neither expected nor received any preferential treatment. Writing about her experiences at the Girls' High School in the years 1891 to 1898, Margaret Milligan said of her father:

> He was both feared and loved, for his justice was strict, yet always mitigated by mercy and humour.[8]

Dr. Milligan was equally strict at home and like the typical Victorian father insisted on a well disciplined household. It was only when he was away from home that the children were able to relax and enjoy themselves. Jean Milligan frequently recalled with affection those Friday evenings at home when free from the strictures of their father, who was visiting his family in Denny, Mrs. Milligan encouraged her children to engage in all kinds of enjoyable activities. There were family plays written by the boys, in which there was a part for everyone. There were lantern slide shows where the appearance of the "ephelant" was greeted with great delight by the young Jean. Much enjoyed also was Mrs. Milligan's story telling, during which something had to be put into the hands of the energetic Jean in order to keep her physically occupied. Dancing, too, was a feature of these evenings of family entertainment; the dances which included the Foursome Reel were taught by Mrs. Milligan. There is no doubt that Mrs. Milligan injected a great deal of fun into the lives of the young Milligans. As will be seen later, Jean Milligan owed a great deal to her mother's influence and example and it has been said, in fact, that "Jean was a kind of replica of her mother."

Mrs. Milligan, Isabella Aitchison before her marriage, was born in 1848 at Fairnington near Roxburgh where her father was a farm steward. Following the death of Isabella's mother in 1850, the Aitchison family was looked after by an unmarried aunt, Margaret Newton of Gattonside. Isabella probably attended the small school situated about one mile from Fairnington, and following the example of her elder sister, Mary, decided to train as a teacher. She was admitted to the Free Church Training College, Glasgow, in January 1868 and completed her training in December 1869.[9]

In addition to her academic achievements, Isabella Aitchison was also a keen and accomplished dancer. In her native Roxburgh she was

Mrs. Isabella Milligan ca.1930.

The Misses Milligan in their garden at Coulter ca.1954. From left to right: Margaret, Jean, Gertrude.

taught to dance by a lady "who came out from Edinburgh" and whose teaching programme no doubt included the country dances as well as the other popular dances of the time. We are told that Isabella had the ability to learn steps and dances very quickly. She had plenty of opportunity to indulge her enthusiasm for dancing because at Fairnington, as elsewhere in the Borders, dancing was an important part of the social life of the farming community. Whilst the stone-floored kitchens were the usual places for small dance parties, a vacant farm worker's cottage, with the permission of the farm steward, often provided space for larger gatherings. It is also said that Isabella gave dance instruction to the seasonal farm workers, mostly Irish, who were employed by her father. Such was her love of dancing that even in old age when no longer able to rise from her chair, Mrs. Milligan still pointed her toes and demonstrated her steps. In later life also her dance knowledge proved very valuable to her daughter Jean who frequently sought her advice when researching dances for publication by the Scottish Country Dance Society. In her accounts of the early days of the Society, Jean Milligan often mentioned the "allemande", which she said was a complete mystery to her until she was enlightened by her mother.

Evidently, Isabella Aitchison was a lively and outward-going young woman, and this may partly explain why in 1870 she left Scotland to take up a teaching appointment in London where her three brothers, Robert, John and Thomas, were already living. It was in London that she married James Milligan who was then headmaster of London Road School, Glasgow; the marriage took place in St. John's Wood English Presbyterian Church, Marlborough Place. The newly married couple made their first Glasgow home at 253 Great Western Road and it was there that their eldest son, John, was born in November 1876.

Jean Callander was the fifth child to be born to James and Isabella Milligan. In view of her remarkable physical stamina in later life, it is surprising to learn that she was not a strong child. Owing, possibly, to the effects of an attack of rheumatic fever, she was not considered fit enough to manage the necessary walk from home to school until the age of nine. Mrs. Milligan supervised her daughter's early education, and consequently Jean was never disadvantaged by her delayed start in regular schooling.

At home with the family, Jean Milligan's childhood and teenage years were very happy. She delighted in the family activities already described and, in later life, remembered with great pleasure the annual family holiday. It was customary for the family to take a house for the summer, and during these excursions they visited Argyll, Fife, Aberdeenshire and Berwickshire. An intriguing glimpse of the Victorian family on holiday is provided by Dr. Milligan's correspondence in preparation for a summer visit to St. Abbs. To Mr.

French at the Wheat Sheaf Inn, Reston, he wrote that he would require a wagonette and a cart to transport eight persons from Reston Station to St. Abbs, and he informed Miss Cowen of 10 New Houses, St. Abbs, that the family would need six beds, half a ton of coal and oil for the lamps.[10] It was during one of these summer holidays that Jean Milligan learned to swim, an activity she enjoyed until age and physical disability made it no longer possible. She became a member of Arlington St. Baths, Glasgow, before the First World War, and the regular dips in the North Sea taken by Miss Milligan and Miss Lilian Ross, although rarely witnessed in later years, were the topics of much discussion at many a St. Andrews Summer School of the Scottish Country Dance Society.

One other place visited by the Milligan family on summer holiday was the Midlothian village of Cousland which was chosen because Mrs. Milligan's cousin, Isabella Barnes, was the wife of the village headmaster. There was great affection and rapport between the two cousins because they had been brought up together at Fairnington by their aunt, Margaret Newton. Mrs. Barnes described to her own daughter some very happy evenings in the kitchen of the Cousland school house. Under Mrs. Milligan's direction, the neighbours were invited to join in an evening of dancing. They danced "Scottish dances" and accompanied themselves by "diddling". In view of Mrs. Milligan's lifelong devotion to dancing, it is not surprising that her daughter Jean should have been equally enthusiastic.

It was not only for her early education and for her love of dancing that Jean Milligan was indebted to her mother. Mrs. Milligan it seems was also very skilled in the kitchen. This was confirmed by a maid who joined the Milligan household before the First World War, and who claimed that she herself had learned a great deal from her kindly employer. Before the maids left the house for their Saturday evening off, they were required to leave out the pans so that Jean and her mother could make tablet. A love of cooking and baking remained with Jean Milligan all her life, and when not working in the kitchen she always kept her hands busy with the knitting pins. The best examples of Miss Milligan's fine handiwork were the knitted shawls, the recipients of which counted themselves very privileged. A proud possessor of such a shawl is the actress and writer, Molly Weir, who wrote, "I am truly honoured, and I will treasure this beautiful hand-worked momento of one of the most remarkable ladies I have known."[11]

At school, as well as at home with the family, Jean Milligan was happy and contented; she frequently recalled her school days as a very enjoyable experience. Although she often acknowledged the academic superiority of her brothers and sisters, describing herself as the "odd one out", her own scholastic achievements were creditable; her

GLASGOW HIGH SCHOOL

FOR GIRLS,

GARNETHILL.

1901-1902.

RECTOR, - JAMES MILLIGAN, M.A., LL.D.

The Session will begin on 2nd September, 1901.

Prospectus of the Glasgow High School for Girls 1901–1902. (*By courtesy of the Mitchell Library, Glasgow*)

Special Group Leaving Certificate included Honours English, Higher French, Higher German, Higher Arithmetic and Lower Mathematics.[12] The approaching end of school days necessitated a decision about what was to follow. With so many teachers in the family, it is hardly surprising that she should have chosen to follow their example. Nor is it surprising that she decided to train as a teacher of physical education. Despite the slow start of her early years, she was soon filled with boundless energy and showed great interest in all forms of

The Gymnasium.

THE system of Gymnastics taught is Ling's Swedish System, of which Madame Bergman Österberg, Principal of the Physical Training College, Dartford Heath, Kent, says that she has "found "none so natural, so carefully progressive, so productive of good " results." "The real aim of gymnastics," she adds, "is health. "Taken in time, they prevent bad habits, they correct bad postures, "and are conducive to correct movement." The Gymnasium is under the charge of Miss Ada Reid, a teacher trained by Madame Österberg, and the course of instruction is carefully graded so as to suit the requirements of girls at every stage of their physical development.

Prospectus of the Glasgow High School for Girls 1901–1902. (*By courtesy of the Mitchell Library, Glasgow*)

physical movement. Miss Milligan remembered experiencing bitter disappointment at being too young to accompany her sister Margaret to a private gymnasium run by Miss K. Campbell of South Park, Hillhead, Glasgow. One of her contemporaries at school, now resident in Australia, describes Jean as a "bright, lively pupil who never hesitated to ask questions of her teachers", and recalls, with envy, her agility on the wall bars in the school gym.

As a pupil at the Girls' High School, Jean Milligan had plenty of opportunity to develop her physical skills, because at the beginning of the session 1900–1 the school acquired a gymnasium and Miss Ada Reid, with a certificate in Ling's Swedish System of Gymnastics, was appointed to take charge of it. Miss Reid had been trained at Dartford College in Kent and her successor, Miss Marion Hunter, came from the same College. At the turn of the century, physical training was a fairly recent addition to the education of girls, and it is greatly to the credit of Dr. James Milligan that he wished to include it in the curriculum of the Girls' High School. He was very keen to promote interest in the work of his physical training teachers. In the session 1903–4, Miss Reid gave an illustrated lecture to the school entitled "Physical Training"; the illustrated lectures were an important feature of school life. On Thursday, 10th March 1905, Dr. Milligan and Miss Hunter arranged a demonstration of Swedish gymnastics for the benefit of those doctors who had daughters at the school and for other parents interested in physical culture.[13] Miss Milligan often spoke of her gratitude to Miss Reid and to Miss Hunter, not only for their inspiration and example, but also because it was through them that she was first introduced to the work of Madame Bergman-Österberg, the owner and Principal of Dartford College.

References

1. *Glasgow Herald*, July 10, 1886, pp. 5, 6, 8.
2. James M. Roxburgh, *The School Board of Glasgow 1873–1919*, pp. 132–42.
3. Register of Students Attending the Glasgow Established Church Training College During the Session 1864, 1865 and 1866, p. 72.
4. *Report of the Religious Institutions in Connection with Wellington Street Congregation, Glasgow. For the Year Ending 30th September 1868*, p. 28; *ibid., For the Year Ending 30th September 1872*, p. 16.
5. *Record of the Ninth Jubilee of the University of Glasgow 1451–1901*, p. 80.
6. *Glasgow Herald*, March 3, 1910.
7. *Hillhead High School Magazine*, Vol. XXIV (Dec., 1948), p. 11.
8. Isabel M. Milligan, "1891–1898," *Girls' High School Magazine*, June 1944 (Jubilee Number), pp. 7–12.
9. Register of Students, Free Church Training College, 1845–1881, Females, Nos. 360, 789.
10. Letters from Mr. James Milligan to Mr. French, Reston, and Miss Cowen, St. Abbs, June 23, 1892, Garnethill Public School, Mr. Milligan's Letter Book (1892), p. 129.
11. Molly Weir, "A Tribute to Miss Milligan," *The People's Journal*, Sept. 9, 1978.
12. *Prospectus of the Glasgow High School for Girls 1905–1906*, p. 32.
13. *Ibid., 1903–1904*, p. 26; letter from Dr. James Milligan, March 17, 1905, Glasgow High School for Girls, Dr. Milligan's Letter Book (1905), p. 394.

2 Dartford

In the autumn of 1905 a College of Hygiene and Physical Training was opened at Dunfermline in Fife, financed by the Carnegie Dunfermline Trust, and a course of training at this new Scottish College, therefore, was a possibility for Jean Milligan. It is clear, however, that Dr. Milligan desired only the acknowledged best for his daughter, and on 13th January 1905, he wrote as follows to Madame Österberg:

> I have a daughter who has been a student under Miss Reid, my late teacher of Swedish Educational Gymnastics, and more recently under Miss Hunter, who succeeded her as Instructress in this school. My daughter has expressed a strong desire to enter into training under you at Dartford Heath. She is in her nineteenth year, is strong and vigorous, and Miss Hunter is of the opinion that she shows a decided aptitude for the work.

A place was reserved for Jean at the College, and as Madame liked her students to be interviewed before they actually enrolled, a meeting was arranged to take place in Edinburgh with Miss Mary Stewart Tait, the College Vice-Principal; ill health prevented Dr. Milligan from taking his daughter to Dartford for the interview as he had planned.[1] The finale to this episode in her life's story was freqently recounted with amusement by Miss Milligan. The interview with Miss Tait took place in the North British Hotel, Edinburgh. The aspiring Dartford student was asked to remove her spectacles in order to read the clock, to which request the Vice-Principal received the unexpected response, "Which clock?" Despite this minor setback, the interview was successful, and in the autumn of 1905 Jean Milligan left her family for the first time in order to begin what she herself described as "the happiest years of my life". During this time she was to meet the lady, who, after her parents and teachers, was the next person to have a profound influence upon her.

Madame Martina Bergman-Österberg is the acknowledged pioneer of physical education and games for girls and women in Great Britain.[2] Until the 1880s there was little provision for this. Madame Bergman-Österberg's outstanding achievement was that she won acceptance of the subject as an essential part of girls' education and in so doing, developed a new profession for women. She was Swedish by birth and was fortunate to have trained at the Royal Central Gymnastic Institute in Stockholm at a time when the son and daughter of the legendary founder of the Institute, Per Henrik Ling, were still actively teaching.

Madame Martina Bergman-Österberg. (*By courtesy of Dartford Faculty of Education and Movement Studies* (*Thames Polytechnic*), *Dartford.*)

The Swedish system of gymnastics, in which Martina Bergman was trained, was designed, according to the Ling philosophy, to achieve the "harmonious development of the whole body". Her appointment by the London School Board in 1881 to the post of Superintendent of Physical Education in Girls' and Infants' Schools gave Miss Bergman the opportunity to promote her ideas in Britain. She realised that soundly trained teachers were essential for success and in 1885 she purchased property in Hampstead and there began the first full-time course in Britain for specialist women teachers of physical education. She married Dr. Österberg in 1886, and in 1895 transferred her College from Hampstead to larger premises at Kingsfield, Dartford Heath, Kent. There Madame Bergman-Österberg offered a two year full-time course in medical gymnastics and teacher training for physical education. Madame demanded the very best from her students and so many girls wished to have the benefit of her training that she could afford to be very selective in those she accepted. Jean Milligan was fortunate to be one of those admitted to Kingsfield.

From the moment of her arrival at Kingsfield, the young Glasgow student was deeply impressed by all that she experienced there. She had a vivid recollection of her first sight of Kingsfield and of Madame; surrounded by the older students dressed in their tunics, the Principal, by then a stocky figure clothed in black, waited to greet the new arrivals. It was Madame Österberg, of course, who made the deepest impression upon her. Jean Milligan wrote the following about the College Principal:

> Madame was a wonderful person. We feared her, but respected and admired her. She was a dedicated person who had the power of imbuing her students with her own enthusiasm. As she said to our section on our last day at College, "Goodbye, my dears, remember it does not matter how good you are you will never be good enough for the profession you have chosen."[3]

Kingsfield College, Dartford, ca. 1914. (*By courtesy of Dartford Faculty of Education and Movement Studies (Thames Polytechnic), Dartford.*)

College discipline was very strict; days and evenings were fully occupied and the students were allowed little free time. Madame could be very kind, but she also could be quite ruthless in her weeding out of unsuitable students. Jean Milligan recalled the story of one such

Kingsfield College, Dart

student, to whom Madame said, "There are things, one of which at least, I must have from a student. First a beautiful body, second, a pleasant and intelligent face and, third, an interesting and alert mind. Now, my dear, you have none of these, and so I will not have you."[4] This insistence on such high standards seems to have had the effect of inspiring even greater loyalty and devotion in those students who successfully stayed the course.

Those who had the opportunity of experiencing Miss Milligan's vital and inspired teaching will no doubt be surprised to learn that during her first year at Dartford she did have difficulties with the practical and teaching aspects of her work; the theoretical and academic work presented no difficulties. Apparently, the problems stemmed from her shyness and nervousness when required to perform before a College tutor. It was the understanding and sympathy of the staff, especially Miss Alma Wickner, that enabled Jean Milligan to overcome her problems during the second year. Very helpful too was another Scottish member of the same section; this was Jane M. MacKay who remained a close friend and who subsequently became Physical Education Organiser in Glasgow.

Dr. Jean Milligan was forever grateful for what she gained from her two years at Dartford. She recognised that Madame Österberg always gave her students "the very best of everything" in their training. Two Surrey County cricketers gave coaching in the nets; a famous Lacrosse coach was brought from London and Miss Peterson, a member of the Ballet of the Royal Opera House in Copenhagen, gave instruction in dance.[5] Dancing, including national dancing, had been introduced by Madame Österberg into her students' training from the earliest days of her College. Jean Milligan particularly enjoyed Miss Peterson's stage dances because, as she said, they appealed to her "very dramatic nature".

Above all it was the example set by the College Principal which Jean Milligan took away from Dartford at the conclusion of her training; it was an example she endeavoured to follow for the rest of her life. In many respects the characters and careers of Martina Bergman-Österberg and Jean Callander Milligan show remarkable similarities. In addition to their ability to fire others with their own enthusiasm, they both demonstrated a great determination to succeed in all that they undertook and could be formidable protagonists of their cause when confronted by opposition. Many years later when commenting on Jean Milligan's "fierce single-mindedness", a friend wrote:

> One was always just a little bit sorry for anyone who held an opinion in any way at variance with her own. It was not the iron hand of dictatorship; it was simply that she believed in her cause with a passion which was matched by no one else's; and besides that the

fact that almost always she knew better – and knew that she knew better.

Jean Milligan came regretfully to the end of the two years of training and left Dartford with a parting gift from Madame. This was a cat which she called Kingsfield in memory of her happy College days. Kinky, as he was affectionately known, had a very long life; he was greatly cosseted by the Milligan family, travelling in style, for example, in a special hamper at the time of the annual summer holiday. Kinky eventually had to be put down but this could only be done when Jean Milligan was away from home.

The first appointment of the newly qualified teacher was in a small private school, Lingholt, at Hindhead in Surrey.[6] The Scottish principal of the school, Miss Macrae Moir, always employed one of "Madame's girls" for physical training. However, in 1909, Jean Milligan was able to return to Glasgow. In the spring of that year she was successful in her application for the post of Assistant Instructress of Physical Training in Dundas Vale Training College, Glasgow.[7]

References

1. Letters from Dr. James Milligan to Madame Bergman-Österberg, Jan. 13, 24, April 19, 1905, Glasgow High School for Girls, Dr. James Milligan's Letter Book (1905), pp. 298, 312, 441.
2. Jonathan May, *Madame Bergman-Osterberg*.
3. Dr. Jean Milligan's Memo Book.
4. *Ibid.*
5. *Ibid.*
6. *Bergman-Österberg College Register of Gymnastic Teachers and Medical Gymnasts 1885–1908.*
7. Glasgow Provincial Committee for the Training of Teachers, Minutes of Meetings, April 30, 1909.

3 Dundas Vale

By 1909 the two Colleges attended by Jean Milligan's parents no longer existed. Since 1906 they had been integral parts of the Glasgow Training Centre, which had been created in that year by the newly formed Glasgow Provincial Committee for the Training of Teachers. The new Training Centre operated in the buildings of the former Church Colleges, now renamed Dundas Vale College and Stow College and also in University classrooms. In the Department of Physical Training, which Jean Milligan joined after the Easter recess of 1909, there were already three Dartford-trained lecturers. There was Miss Audrey Ash and on a one year appointment terminating in September 1909, Miss Ada Reid, Jean Milligan's former teacher from the Girls' High School. The Head of Department was Miss Olive Smith who had previously taught crippled children in Glasgow University's Queen Margaret College Settlement and instructed the women prisoners of Duke Street Prison in gymnastics; her work, it is said, was "necessarily done on original lines".[1] The physical training of the male students at Dundas Vale was the responsibility of Lieutenant Street.

Dundas Vale College, 1837–1921.

Then in her twenty-third year, Jean Milligan was not much older than many of the students at the time of her appointment to Dundas Vale; dressed in a gym tunic, she was on occasions mistaken for a student herself. Only seven months younger than her instructress, a student of 1909 has provided a glimpse of Miss Milligan at work during her first term. One day an Inspector arrived, ostensibly to assess the work of her students, but no doubt to investigate the potential of the new member of staff. As was usual with the Swedish system of exercises, the girls were arranged in lines in the gymnasium, leaders at the front; our student was one of those leaders. The Inspector called on the students one after the other to give commands for an exercise, with no very brilliant results. Miss Milligan, with a list of class members in her hand, was then seen to place her finger under a certain name and heard to say quietly, "Try this one." "This one," of course, proved to be one of the most promising teachers in the section. Not only had Miss Milligan's students, and later her country dancers, to be good, they had to be seen (and heard) to be good.

In later life, Miss Milligan often told how at the beginning of her College career, she went out to primary and secondary schools in Glasgow to teach classes of younger Scottish children. A lady who, with her three sisters, was among those school children, has given the following delightful account of the visits:

My own memory of Miss Milligan and her lessons is so clear that I often recall with deep affection how we would go to the front gate every afternoon about three o'clock to await her coming. After her

Jordanhill Training College, 1921.

(*Pictures by courtesy of Jordanhill College of Education*)

Training College Hockey Club, 1913. Back row (left to right): J. Irving, N. MacLean, R. Brown, Miss Jean Milligan (President), J. Martin, A. Smith, N. Neilson. Front row (left to right): S. Kerr, A. Black, E. Broad, M. M'Gibbon, J. Jack. (*Picture by courtesy of Jordanhill College of Education*)

"drill" lesson came the period of Scottish country dancing which we loved and enjoyed so much. Following on the formal intruction, Miss Milligan would stand at the piano, facing the pupils and playing for our dancing. Not a moment of the period was wasted. A high standard was expected of us and we responded with the greatest respect and affection.

The new Physical Training Instructress entered into the work of the College with characteristic enthusiasm. The Milligan maid, mentioned in the first chapter, describes her at this time as "aye fleein' with a hockey stick under her arm." Miss Milligan, it seems, was particularly keen to develop games as part of the physical training syllabus and, in consequence, must have welcomed the purchase by the Provincial Committee in 1912 of the Jordanhill Mansion and its extensive grounds. Although not actually ready for occupation until 1921, the acquisition of Jordanhill enabled the Committee to fulfil its plans for the provision of a new College building. Immediately, however, Jordanhill provided much needed playing fields and Miss Milligan now had a fine hockey pitch with a good pavilion, an asset to the College Hockey Club which, in 1912, joined the Scottish Ladies' Hockey Association.[2]

Miss Milligan was also very enthusiastic about netball, the game introduced into Britain in the 1890s from the United States via Madam Österberg's College. The Dartford-trained teachers in and around Glasgow formed a netball team which often played against teams of senior school pupils. It was at such netball matches that a

GENERAL SCOTTISH NEWS

THE BELTANE SOCIETY FESTIVAL.

The festival of folk-song, drama, dance, and children's games, promoted by the Beltane Society was continued in the Athenæum Hall, Glasgow, on Saturday evening. Though the hall was not quite filled, there was a good attendance. The abundant and quaint fare provided was heartily appreciated by the audience, who insisted on encores to such an extent that the programme was prolonged considerably beyond the advertised hour. The entertainment opened with a dance of the old-fashioned "country" type, danced by young men and maidens in old-world rustic garb. The gracefulness and rhythm which characterised this and the subsequent dances—"Blue Bonnets," "Flowers o' Edinburgh," and others—made one regret that the modern ball-room knows them no more. Several singing games were performed by a large band of bright little folk. The soloists were Miss Jenny Taggart and Mr Charles Tree. Miss Taggart's cultured voice was heard to fine advantage in the round dozen or so examples she rendered from the old-time minstrelsy, whether in the haunting Gaelic fragments, or in the plaintive and love-breathing Lowland melodies. Mr Tree also selected pieces representative of Gaelic and Lowland sentiment in song, his renderings being delightfully expressive, particularly in "Green grow the Rashes, O," and "The Forlorn Lass." Fine feeling was put into his singing of "Maiden of Morven." Mr J. D. Macdonald performed the Highland dances with grace, and Misses Florence Clark and Jean Milligan gave an admirable representation of morris dancing. Opportunity was taken by Mr Graham Price to explain to those present the objects of the Beltane Society, which are to revive an interest in folklore, dances, singing games, and kindred subjects.

Glasgow Herald, **Monday, 28th October 1912.** (*By courtesy of the Mitchell Library, Glasgow*)

pupil of Hamilton Academy, who later became a student at Dundas Vale, first met Miss Milligan.

Those people who met Jean Milligan during the years before the First World War have provided a picture of a young woman enjoying life to the full, applying herself wholeheartedly to her professional work and pursuing her personal interests with equal zest.

In view of her interest in Scottish country dances, first stimulated by her mother, it was natural that Miss Milligan should be closely associated with the Beltane Society, formed in Glasgow in 1912. The aims of this Society were "to cultivate among the younger generation a knowledge of Scottish folk songs, ballads, dances and singing games, to maintain all the national customs and quaint ceremonies, and to increase interest in Scottish history, legend and myth by means of simple plays."[3] During its regrettably short existence, for it did not survive the outbreak of the First World War, the Society arranged a series of lectures, concerts and festivals to illustrate many facets of Scottish culture. Among the items performed at the first such festival in the Athenaeum in Glasgow in October 1912 were the traditional Scottish country dances "Blue Bonnets", "Flowers of Edinburgh" and "The Nut". Commenting on these dances, a *Glasgow Herald* account of the Festival says that they, "like other country dances favoured by our forefathers, have been elbowed out of the modern ballroom by ragtime, two-steps, up to date waltzes and other latterday specimens of the terpsichorean art." The *Glasgow Herald* also reported that "Misses Florence Clark and Jean Milligan gave an admirable representation of morris dancing."[4]

Like all dedicated teachers, Miss Milligan did not confine herself to working within statutory hours. Students trained from as early as 1910 have spoken with gratitude of the class for former students to which they were delighted to return when their student days were over. Meeting on Wednesdays, just after school hours, this extension of Miss Milligan's work, affectionately known as "The Old Students' Class", probably flourished until the beginning of the Second World War. It was, of course, a purely voluntary activity undertaken by the ex-students and their teacher. No fees were charged and Miss Milligan looked for no monetary reward though she occasionally accepted a present from the grateful members. Since the class lasted for so many years, accounts by members of what was taught by Miss Milligan have varied. At times, it is said, the class consisted of "drill" for half the time, and dancing for the remainder. In addition to Scottish dances, there were other national dances, minuets, and gavottes and many "attractive little dances" which were very useful in school. Included, too, were team and singing games for use with pupils.

All members of the Old Students' Class are unanimous in their praise of the dances composed by Miss Milligan herself. These were miniature ballets, often illustrating themes from nature such as "The Seasons" and "Fireflies", while other intriguing subjects included "Dancing through the Ages", "Mayday Revels", "The Princess who never Smiled" and an imaginative interpretation of a game of whist. A student whose training began in 1922 and who was immediately recruited to play the piano when her talents as a pianist were discovered, has described Miss Milligan's individual choreographic style as follows:

> She would "build" her dances like a pattern on a carpet, saying, "I'm going from here to here, see how much music I need" or "Give me sixteen bars" and she would see how far the music would take her. In that way, counting, stopping, recounting and altering, she completed the pattern.

Another class member recalls an occasion when Miss Milligan, "in her short blue gym tunic, with black shoes and stockings and her lanky straight hair pulled back in a bun by very large, straight-legged hairpins," was demonstrating a step between two rows of kneeling dancers. As she danced down between them, the hairpins, proving of little use, cascaded to the floor; she gleaned a harvest of pins as she danced back again.

The yearly highlight of the Old Students' Class was a display which was staged originally in the Queen's Rooms, Charing Cross and later in the McLellan Galleries or the Lyric Theatre. The proceeds from these performances were donated to one of the many charities dear to Miss Milligan's heart. The items on every programme were always suitably dressed, wigs and period costume for minuets and gavottes and such imaginative ensembles as a grey tunic with violet shoes and stockings for the character of "The Shortest Day" in the presentation of "The Seasons". Like most creative artists, Miss Milligan was never satisfied with her productions but kept on altering and improving them, even having last-minute thoughts about costume. On one occasion, the dancers having each bought a pair of white cotton stockings and dyed one red, the other yellow, were devastated at the dress rehearsal to be told, "Not at all! Both must be yellow!" Tears flowed freely but next day all stockings were yellow. Rehearsals, too, are known to have been disrupted when one Maypole dancer got everyone so constantly tangled that she had to be transferred to a less intricate dance.

Miss Milligan not only devised but also danced in many of these productions. In a programme of 1914, she and her partner, Miss F. Clark, performed a Gypsy Dance in each half of the programme, the first with castanets, the second with tambourines and in "The Seasons" she danced the part of "Summer".[5] At one performance Miss Milligan had a slight mishap. While she was dancing, the pince-nez she then wore fell on to the stage and only her acrobatic expertise and strong sense of rhythm enabled her to retrieve them without losing more than a beat or two of the music.

It is interesting to note that at least one Lyric Theatre display was attended by Mrs. Milligan. One of the dancers that night, now resident in Canada, remembers that she and her friends were warned by Miss Milligan that they had "better be good" because "my mother knows every step of all the dances." Last minute practices took place behind the scenes and seemingly, all was well.

Whilst in her teaching the young Miss Milligan showed a keen interest in all aspects of movement, games, gymnastics and dancing, it was inevitable even at this early stage in her career that Scottish country dancing should have featured prominently in her work with children in school, with the Beltane Society, with her students in College and with the Old Students' Class. A member of that class, just before the First World War, has said that Miss Milligan taught Petronella, the Duke of Perth and the Foursome and Eightsome Reels. This lady was a member of a team of Miss Milligan's "old" students who, clad in tartan skirts, travelled to such places as Greenock to give demonstrations at the famous Burns Club there. This team also gave a demonstration to the Glasgow Burns Club, and on that occasion Miss Milligan asked each of the girls to bring a male partner. One dancer

A demonstration by members of Miss Milligan's Old Students' Class ca.1914.

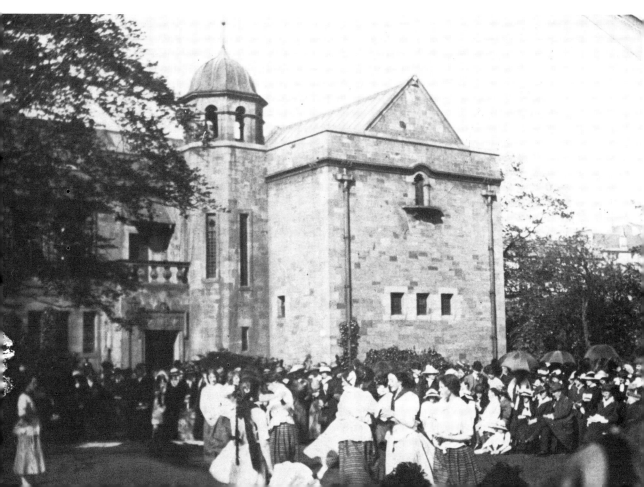

brought her "sulky" brother, who immediately, it seems, fell under the Milligan spell; in preparation for the event, he practised his steps assiduously, admiring his own efforts in a wall mirror from the top of the dining room table!

Undoubtedly the Old Students' Class provided the nucleus of the later Scottish Country Dance Society and from it were recruited the Society's founder members and first teachers. One such early Society member said that it was "easy to pass from the Old Students' Class to the Country Dance Class in 1923."

A First World War student now living in America recalls a country dance lesson in memorable circumstances. Her class was in the Dundas Vale gymnasium with Miss Milligan "practising our Scottish steps" one morning when, suddenly, the door burst open and an excited party of young men from the University rushed in bringing word of the newly signed Armistice – it was 11th November 1918. The students immediately changed into outdoor clothes and dashed along Sauchiehall Street waving flags and cheering. There is no mention of Miss Milligan's joining the exuberant crowd but no doubt that day would have sombre thoughts for her, bringing back memories of her war service in Malta.

It was in October 1915 that Miss Smith and Miss Milligan were given permission by the Glasgow Provincial Committee to go on war service.[6] Miss Smith went to Salonica and died there in October 1916 after contracting malaria; she was buried with military honours at Salonica.[7] Miss Milligan was drafted as a VAD to Malta and sailed on a hospital ship in January 1916, her destination Valetta.[8]

The Voluntary Aid Detachment was composed of auxiliary nurses, under army discipline and paid by the army. Their services were greatly needed in Malta where the hospitals received large numbers of casualties from Gallipoli in 1915 and from Salonica in 1916. A report on the work of the VADs in Malta stated:

> Without the assistance of the VAD nurses, the nursing could not have been carried on effectively. Many of them are ladies of conspicuous refinement and culture, and some, to our knowledge, came out to help to nurse the sick and wounded at considerable personal sacrifice.[9]

Miss Milligan described the Valetta hospital as being in the shape of a cross, with one hundred patients in each ward. The ward to which she was assigned was entirely devoted to soldiers invalided from Salonica; they were mainly victims of frost-bite caused by excessive cold but there were also cases of trench fever and malaria. At first sight of this suffering, the newly recruited VAD broke down and wept but pulled herself together and soon became absorbed in her work. Her training in medical gymnastics and massage at Dartford now proved to be an invaluable asset. She has told of one young man who had lost half of each foot and had no more interest in life. After much encouraging, coaxing and bullying, he finally made the effort and learned to walk again.

Miss Milligan spoke of the Valetta hospital as "a happy place, where the soldiers were glad to be." When she herself developed a cough, one young lad with TB insisted on saving some of his medicine for "Nurse Milligan". Discovering this infringement of discipline, the Sister not surprisingly objected strongly and put a peremptory stop to it, but for the rest of her life the VAD was to remember, with gratitude, the boy's concern for her. Years later, with her accustomed verve, Miss Milligan used to say, "I love hospitals." She was a good nurse, and many a country dancer at Summer School and elsewhere has had good reason to be grateful to her for sympathy and practical help in times of emergency.

On the expiry of her term of service in Malta, Miss Milligan applied to have her leave of absence from Dundas Vale extended. This was refused and she was obliged to return to her teaching duties in October 1916.[10] Back in Glasgow, she returned to her work with undiminished enthusiasm. On the resignation of Miss Audrey Ash, who had succeeded Miss Smith as Head of Department in October 1916, Miss Milligan was offered the post in Sepember 1917. It is recorded that her acceptance was accompanied by a strong protest about her new salary; at £130 per annum it was only £30 more than she had received as an Assistant in 1909.[11]

After the War, in addition to her duties as Principal Instructress in Physical Training, Miss Milligan continued with characteristic vigour to organise the annual Gala Days at Jordanhill. The first of these had been held in 1913; on the lawn behind the Mansion House, according to *The Training College Magazine*, "a number of senior ladies evoked the praises of all who saw their splendid exhibition of Swedish gymnastics," whilst the entertainment on the tennis court by the folk dancers "was undoubtedly the finest on the programme."[12] The Gala Days, always held toward the end of June, became an institution and under Miss Milligan's direction flourished for many years, making valuable contributions to numerous charities.

As well as sports events and fund raising stalls, at Gala Day there was always a dancing display devised by Miss Milligan. A newly appointed member of the College Staff first witnessed such a display in 1944 and these are his recorded impressions:

The College lawn was surrounded by spectators and in the centre a game of whist was in progress with students as playing cards. Miss Milligan was in charge and in her element. Looking back on that day, I realise the whole affair conveyed a great deal about Miss

Milligan. She was responsible for the display and obviously dominated the scene. The participants were beautifully turned out, very well drilled, and the whole thing executed with panache.

For Miss Milligan, for the student participants and for other College staff, Gala Days could be days of hidden tensions. On at least one occasion even the redoubtable Miss Milligan succumbed to the anxieties of the day. It was on her last Gala Day in 1948, the year of her retirement. Rain had forced the dancing display indoors and on discovering that the student pianist, with the piano key and the music in her possession, was nowhere to be found, Miss Milligan was reduced to tears. Composure, however, was quickly recovered and in the event all was well.

Jean Milligan was always very proud of her College. In Dundas Vale and from 1921 in its new home at Jordanhill, she gave great loyalty and devoted service. From her earliest years as a College lecturer her interest in her students was lively and constant. That it was enduring is in no way better demonstrated than by her lifelong association with the "F Section" of 1917–19. Although much reduced in numbers now, that Section has held a reunion every year since its members completed their training. At the invitation of her "old" students, Miss Milligan, except when prevented from doing so by travels abroad or by ill health, attended every reunion until 1978. Having just attended the reunion that year, she wrote her note of thanks on 23rd March, and said:

> How I enjoyed meeting the "girls". I feel highly honoured that you all remember me. I do hope you keep well and that we will have the happiness of meeting again, but, alas, I at least am getting very old, though I do not feel so.

The faithful Section were not to meet Miss Milligan again, but with what pride must the few remaining Dundas Vale students look back on sixty years of unbroken friendship.

References

1. *Magazine of the Bergman Österberg Union of Trained Gymnastic Teachers*, Vol. 1. No. 1. (Jan., 1917), p. 12.
2. *The Training College Magazine*, Dec., 1912, p. 23.
3. *Glasgow Herald Year Book 1913*, p. 288.
4. *Glasgow Herald*, Oct. 24, 28, 1912.
5. RSCDS Log, Vol. 1.
6. Glasgow Provincial Committee for the Training of Teachers, Minutes of Meetings, Oct. 4, 1915.
7. *Ibid.*, Dec. 8, 1916.
8. *Ibid.*, Jan. 27, 1916.

9. *Reports by the Joint War Committee and the Joint War Finance Committee of the British Red Cross Society and the Order of St. John of Jerusalem in England 1914–1919*, p. 384.

10. Glasgow Provincial Committee for the Training of Teachers, Minutes of Meetings, Sept. 5, 1916.

11. *Ibid.*, Sept. 21, Nov. 26, 1917.

12. *The Training College Magazine*, June, 1913, p. 100.

4 The Scottish Country Dance Society

In June 1923, protesting against the unemployment, deprivation and ugliness of the post-war world, the novelist Winifred Holtby wrote to a friend as follows:

> We want drill instructors and folk dancers ... we want ballet dancers and singing masters who will not be afraid of holding classes at street corners if necessary.[1]

Not long after that letter was written, two ladies in Scotland got together to work on those lines, if not literally (though one of them was no doubt capable of it) certainly metaphorically, for that was when

Miss Milligan and Mrs. Stewart, St. Andrews, 1927.

Mrs. Stewart and Miss Milligan started the movement which is now worldwide and is known as "The Royal Scottish Country Dance Society".

Mrs. Ysobel Stewart of Fasnacloich, at that time a Commissioner of Girl Guides in Ayrshire, had learned Scottish country dancing in her youth and was teaching it to her Guides as enthusiastically as Miss Milligan was to her students. Mrs. Stewart felt strongly that an effort should be made to preserve the old dances, but, since she was not a professional teacher, thought it advisable to seek help. She approached Mr. James Michael Diack of Patersons, the music publishers in Glasgow. Mr. Diack's son describes that first contact thus:

> I remember so well the day when Mrs. Stewart called at my father's office in Glasgow and told him about her idea of a Scottish Country Dance Society. He at once thought of Jean Milligan, whom he knew very well through his work as Superintendent of Music in schools. He introduced the two of them, I think the same day, and they were both very grateful.

Shortly after the first meeting between Mrs. Stewart and Miss Milligan, a notice was inserted in the *Glasgow Herald* inviting all interested in "Scots Country Dances" to attend a meeting in the Athenaeum, Glasgow, at 5 o'clock on Monday, 26th November, 1923. Miss Milligan often used to tell how she and Mrs. Stewart whispered dubiously to each other, "Do you think any one will come?" In fact, twenty-seven people attended and from such small beginnings the Scottish Country Dance Society began to grow.

The inaugural meeting, chaired by Mr. F. H. Bisset, Chairman of

Glasgow Herald, **Monday, 26th November 1923.** (*By courtesy of the Mitchell Library, Glasgow*)

ANNUAL MEETING, CENTRAL HALLS, BATH STREET, GLASGOW, TO-NIGHT. at 8 p.m. Members are urgently asked to be present, as the business is very important.

SCOTS COUNTRY DANCES.

A MEETING of all interested in above will be held in the ATHENÆUM, ST GEORGE'S PLACE, ROOM 17, TO-NIGHT, at 5 o'clock.

THE CHURCHES AND NO-LICENCE.

THE TRUTH ABOUT
PROHIBITION IN AMERICA.

PUBLIC MEETINGS
Will be held as undernoted:
TO-DAY (MONDAY), 26th NOVEMBER,
In Y.M.C.A. HALL, EGLINTON TOLL.
SPEAKERS:—
Rev. JOSEPH JOHNSTON, M.A., Edinburgh.

the Federation of Musical Festivals, decided to form a Society. It then appointed an interim Executive Committee, which included Miss Milligan, Miss Lilian Ross, Mr. Diack, Mr. Bisset and Mrs. Stewart, as Honorary Secretary. The annual membership fee of 5s. was fixed, at which modest sum it remained until 1967 when it was raised to 7s. 6d.

The interim Committee met for the first time in Glasgow on 19th December 1923 and at that meeting Research and Publications sub-committees were formed. Miss Milligan was a member of the latter and was included with Mrs. Blackie and Mrs. Stewart in the Dancing Committee formed to arrange teaching in Glasgow and the West; other two Dancing Committees were established for Edinburgh and the East and for the North and Grampians. It was decided at the same meeting that twelve dances should be published as soon as possible.

Work was started immediately on Book 1, Miss Milligan and Mrs. Stewart each contributing six dances from their previous knowledge. Mr. Diack arranged the music and Patersons, by agreement with the new Society, undertook to meet the entire cost of the first publication. To Miss Milligan fell the task of preparing the dances for publication, so she gathered together a group from her Old Students' Class. One of the group describes the event in these words:

> I was lucky to have been picked for the team with which Miss Milligan worked out the dances for Book 1. I can clearly picture the scene in the gymnasium of Dundas Vale, where Lord James Stewart Murray and Mrs. Stewart came to watch and approve our efforts.

At the end of January 1924, Book 1 of the Scottish Country Dance Society was issued and, according to the first Annual Report, 1,165 copies were sold.[2] That this was possible so soon after the inauguration of the Society is a tribute not only to the burning enthusiasm of Miss Milligan herself but also to the charismatic personality which, all her life, was to inspire others to share her zeal.

One of these was Lord James Stewart Murray, Duke of Atholl from 1942, who became the Society's Chairman at the first Annual General Meeting in November 1924; from the beginning, he was also its President, an office which he retained until his death in 1957. Commenting on the Society's debt to Lord James, Miss Milligan said, "... he practically never missed a meeting of any sort, and brought a great wealth of information to us."[3] He had an unrivalled knowledge of the history of his native Perthshire and was an authority on Highland dress and on traditional Scottish music and dance. He danced all his life, having been taught by one of the famous itinerant teachers, "Dancie" Neill of Forfar. When in his seventies, he once electrified the Society members at an Annual General Meeting by rising from his seat on the platform to dance the solo Russian step commonly called

Scottish Country Dance Society.

A meeting was held in the Athenaem, Glasgow on 26th November 1923.

Present. Mr F. H. Bisset (in the Chair)

Mr J. Michael Diack,   Miss J. M. MacKay
Miss Margaret Hopkins,   Miss Drummond
Miss Helen Martin,   Mr J. H. Lauder,
Miss M. E. M. Main,   Mr J. D. Elder
Miss J. M. Loudon,   Miss M. S. Warnock
Mr J. S. Gregson   Miss Helen MacDonald
Major J. C. Stewart   Mrs J. C. Stewart
Miss M. Montgomerie.   Miss A. Wordie
Miss M. F. Robertson.   Miss M. L. Ross.
Miss E. M. MacLellan,   Miss Jean Lang
Miss Margaret MacLeod,   Miss N. C. MacMillan
Miss M. E. B. MacMurtrie   Miss Jessie Cochrane
Mr R. P. Thomson,   Miss Jean Milligan

Apologies for absence were read from — The Lady Helen Tod
          The Lady Margaret MacRae

Extract from the Minutes of the Inaugural Meeting of the
Scottish Country Dance Society, 26th November 1923.

26th November 1923.

Major the Lord James Stewart Murray,
Mrs Burnley Campbell of Ormidale
Mrs Blackie   Miss Blair
Miss Campbell of Inverneill, Mrs J. Cox.
Miss L. Dalmahoy,   Miss Logan-Home.
Miss Moorhouse,   Colonel J. D. Boswell.
Mr R. F. Graham,   Captain Colin MacRae
Captain J. D. Ramsay,   Mr J. E. Shaw
Mr William Donald.   Miss Lander,
Miss Allan,   Miss Sharp
Miss Hair   Miss Cameron (Ardoch)
Mr V. E. Gooderson.

The Chairman in addressing the
meeting set forward the proposal
to form a society, having as its
aims the following objects —
1. To practise and preserve
   Country Dances, as danced in Scotland
2. To collect old books, manuscripts
   or pictures descriptive or
   illustrative of Scottish dances.
3. To publish, from time to time,

Scottish Country Dance Society.

━━

The above Society was formed in November, 1923, with the following objects:—

1. To practice and preserve Country Dances as danced in Scotland.

2. To collect old books, manuscripts and pictures illustrative of Scottish Dances.

3. To publish, from time to time, descriptions of Country Dances, with diagrams and music in simple form, at a moderate price.

━━

Members of Committee. 1924=25

Lord James Stewart Murray (*Chairman*).
Brigadier General Ronald Cheape (*Vice-Chairman*).
Miss Jean Milligan.
Miss L. Dalmahoy.
Miss Ruth Berry.
Miss M. L. Ross.
Colonel J. D. Boswell.
J. Bartholomew.
G. Macpherson Grant.
J. M. Diack.
Mrs Stewart, 3 Park Circus, Ayr (*Secretary*).
N. H. Wilson, British Linen Bank, Ayr (*Treasurer*).

The Annual Subscription for members is 5/-, and each member receives a free copy of one of the Dance Books.

Scottish Country Dance Society.

SEASON 1924-25.
Glasgow Branch.

━━

The Committee have arranged to hold the following Classes for tuition in the Dances contained in Books I. and II.

CLASSES FOR TEACHERS

For BOOK I—Four Lessons.

Place—Dundas Vale School, Cowcaddens.
Commencing on Thursday, 22nd January, 7-8.30.
Fees for Members of the Society, 4/-. Non-Members, 6/6.

For BOOK II—Six Lessons.

Place—Dundas Vale School, Cowcaddens.
Commencing on Tuesday, 27th January, 5.30-7.
Fees for Members of the Society, 6/-. Non-Members 8/6.

Miss Milligan hopes to take both of these Classes.

Other Classes may be arranged if found necessary.

Enquiries should be addressed to Mr. R. Percy Thomson, 134 St. Vincent Street, Glasgow, or to Paterson, Sons & Co., Ltd., 152 Buchanan Street, Glasgow.

A Glasgow Branch Syllabus, 1924-5.

the "Cobbler's Step". Those who heard Miss Milligan's "talks" will recall that she often said that it was Lord James who continually urged the Society "to remain true to tradition." He was also firmly convinced that Scottish country dancing, with its universal appeal, could help to heal the class divisions which had developed in towns and cities; this was often the theme of his Presidential remarks at Annual General Meetings. Despite failing health in later years, until the end of his life, Lord James maintained a close interest in the work of the Society and of his local Perth and Perthshire Branch.

Within a month of the publication of Book 1, Miss Milligan proposed that a class should be started immediately in Glasgow. A course of four lessons was arranged, the fee to be 2s. 6d. for members of the Society, 5s. for non-members, and Miss Milligan to teach free of charge. The class, with over sixty members, was successful; a class in Edinburgh, unfortunately, was not so satisfactory.[4] The success of the Glasgow class was assured by Miss Milligan's former students who flocked to it in large numbers. The class met on a Tuesday at half-past five, a time very suitable for teachers. The direct descendant of this pioneer class still meets on the same day at the same time. In its sixty-year history it has had only two regular teachers, Miss Milligan and Miss Florence Adams.

At these early classes there were very few men. Sixty years ago, there was a sad reason for this. During the First World War, a whole generation of young men had been wiped out, leaving thousands of women in the position aptly described as "war widows who had never been married". Looking back to the Society's early days, Miss Milligan once said, "I thought, 'Here's something these hundreds of unmarried women can do, something that's fun and doesn't need men!' "[5] A very Milliganesque remark! The lady who told her, "I thought I'd never dance again," voiced the gratitude of all those women, widowed and single, who were partnerless and would have felt de trop, if not unwelcome, at an ordinary dance, especially in the 1920s and 30s when it was the custom for couples to dance together right through the programme.

Another of Miss Milligan's later comments on the early work of the Society was that it was not necessary "to revive a dead dog, just resuscitate an ailing one." In 1923 Scottish country dancing was indeed in poor health. The few dances such as the Eightsome Reel, Petronella, Strip the Willow and Duke of Perth which still appeared on dance programmes were usually the occasions for rowdy behaviour. Before joining one of these dances, the girls often removed cherished jewellery which they left with a less intrepid friend on the side-lines until the fray was over. As all the sets of Eightsome Reels in a hall very rarely finished at the same time, the band simply kept on playing until the last set gave in.

From the beginning, therefore, Mrs. Stewart and Miss Milligan were determined that Scottish country dancing should be brought back to the ballroom in a refined and sociable manner. Miss Milligan once said that they were "teaching methods which were one hundred years old." It is interesting to note that through her first teacher, her mother, she did have a possible direct link with the early nineteenth century when dancing was a disciplined and elegant pastime. The lady from Edinburgh who taught Mrs. Milligan in Roxburgh, probably during the 1850s, could have learned her dancing twenty or thirty years before. Whilst wishing to restore elegance to country dancing in the ballroom, Miss Milligan always insisted that gaiety and a happy spirit were equally desirable. The resourceful lady later coined the inimitable description of correct Scottish country dancing, "controlled abandon", and in her book, *Won't You Join the Dance*, wrote:

> ... dancing is a joyous thing and must never become so drilled and detailed as to lose the natural gay social spirit, which should be aroused in the dancers by the lively movements of these national dances and the stimulus of their gay, Scottish music.[6]

Another of her well known sayings, "Dance with your soul," summed up a firmly held belief that a lively and spontaneous response to the music was just as important as correct dancing technique.

To the charges of invention by the Society in those early days, Miss Milligan responded with vigorous denials. After much research, she argued, the aim was to adopt steps and formations in their earliest known form and to achieve a measure of standardisation which would allow country dancers to enjoy their dances wherever they might be. In this connection, Miss Milligan enjoyed telling the story of the two-handed poussette. An old man on the Duke of Atholl's estate objected to the two-handed version insisting, "We've aye done it gruppit." He was referring to the practice of taking waltz grasp. The Society's rejection of this method, however, was vindicated when there came to light a letter, dated 25th January 1802, in which Mr. A. Smith of Hamilton clearly describes the two-handed poussette.[7]

The revival of interest in the country dances ensured that new life was given to Scotland's traditional dance music. In selecting tunes for their dances, the co-founders in the early days received invaluable help from such enthusiasts as Mrs. Annie Shand of Aberdeen and Lady Dorothea Ruggles Brise, sister of Lord James Stewart, who in her lifetime built up a fine collection of printed sources of traditional music. When that help was no longer available there was great reliance upon Miss Milligan's knowledge and tireless investigation. Before the publication of each new book, she would spend hours at the piano, sifting through old collections to find suitable alternative tunes for dances with their own tunes or to find tunes for dances for which there was no music. All over the world, hundreds of musicians as well as dancers should remember with gratitude the work of Miss Milligan and her enthusiastic helpers throughout the years.

With Book 1 published and the first classes started, the popularity of Scottish country dancing spread very quickly and by 1925, the Society had six branches; they were Glasgow, Edinburgh, Aberdeen, Dundee, Greenock and Perthshire. Either Miss Milligan or Mrs. Stewart, sometimes both, would be present at the birth of each branch, Miss Milligan often taking a team of dancers or teaching the first lesson. Ever spreading interest meant an increasing demand for classes and, consequently, for teachers. In June 1924, to ensure maintenance of the aims of the founders and of the teaching standards of Miss Milligan,

Mr. Diack proposed the introduction of an examination for a teaching certificate.[8] Lord James, Miss Milligan and Mrs. Stewart conducted the first examination of thirty-three successful candidates in Glasgow in October 1924 and in the following month they examined four successful teachers in Edinburgh.[9] In Glasgow the first candidates were mostly from Miss Milligan's Old Students' Class. The first examination was based on Book 1 and because that contained no strathspey dances, a further examination had to be arranged on the publication of Book 2 in 1925. Only after success in both these tests was a teacher considered capable of maintaining the required standard.

At the Society's first meeting in November 1923, Mr. Bisset had said that Musical Festivals would be an appropriate means of promoting country dancing and through his good offices, classes in Scottish country dancing were very soon introduced into the major Scottish Festivals. Mr. Bisset was editor of a series of *Festival Booklets*, which aimed to improve standards in each of the fields of musical festival competition. In December 1924, Miss Milligan was invited to contribute to this series for Scottish country dancing. In this, her first venture into authorship, she produced a booklet full of such valuable hints on the subject that a copy was sent to each member of the Country Dance Society and an enlarged edition was issued again in the early 1930s. Adjudicating the Scottish country dance classes in Musical Festivals gave Miss Milligan another outlet for her drive and enthusiasm. As in her other public activities, she showed great skill. She could be critical or full of praise and at times infuriatingly unpredictable but her intention always was to encourage and to entertain; "it must be constructive, helpful criticism, in which there is no hurt," she said.[10] Many of today's Scottish country dancers first met Miss Milligan when competing as children in festivals where invariably they fell under her spell. A lady, now resident in Canada, who danced as a child in the team from Shields Road School, Glasgow, writes:

> We competed at St. Andrews Halls and I shall always remember Miss Milligan, who was the adjudicator; she gave us lots of praise but lots of advice too. Once, during the General Strike in 1926, we were entered to compete, and – panic! no trams or buses, so over the ferry at Clyde Street, and there were we, marching up to the competition. We were all so keen in those days.

Miss Milligan's adjudicating assignments in those early years are remembered for other reasons by her College students. When travelling to the Dumfries Festival, for example, she would cram two or three local girls from the College hostel into her car so that they could have an extra weekend at home. Probably students from other

A group at St. Andrews Summer School, 1933. Back row (left to right): Miss M. Dow, Miss M. W. Kenyon, Miss A. Anderson, Miss E. M. Dunbar, Miss M. L. Ross. Middle row (left to right): Mrs. P. Thomson, Miss Milligan, Miss Douglas-Brown. Front row (left to right): Miss M. Maxwell, Miss W. E. Forgan (SCDS Sec.).

regions also will recall with gratitude these much appreciated good turns.

With the growing popularity of country dancing in the later 1920s, the next step taken by Miss Milligan and Mrs. Stewart was to inaugurate a Summer School. The first School took place in 1927, for one week only. The venue was St. Andrews and, except for the years 1940 to 1944, it has been the highlight of the Society's annual activities ever since. The Summer School was the love of Miss Milligan's life and there is no greater testimony of her devotion to it than the fact that at the time of her fatal collapse in 1978 all arrangements for the month at St. Andrews that summer were entirely complete. She was quite clear about the purpose of the Summer School as is evident from her words to the staff and students of her last Summer School in 1977:

> Summer School was started to maintain standards worldwide. It is a privilege to attend Summer School and should make us not merely loyal, but dedicated to the aims of the Royal Scottish Country Dance Society.

Only those who attended Summer School in the early days know how delightfully friendly and informal were these Schools under the directorship of a young Miss Milligan who could and did enter with zest into every activity. As in later years, at her morning class, she taught the dances for each new book as it was published but she was also in charge of the social dancing which took place every evening except Sunday. On these occasions she exchanged a lot of good-humoured badinage with the students, for whom the highlight of social dancing was to be partnered by Miss Milligan. The parties which flourished after social dancing were small and totally non-alcoholic. Miss Milligan liked to be invited and when present, invariably taking the lead, would be certain to contribute greatly to the spirit of fun. Friday evening ceilidhs were introduced into Summer School in more recent times. These events, attended by the whole School, always gave Miss Milligan a great deal of enjoyment.

Owing to the missionary zeal of Miss Milligan and her helpers, the valuable work of the Scottish Country Dance Society was beginning to be recognised by other organisations. In 1928, the organisers of the ambitious Pageant of Glasgow sought the help of the Society and it was agreed that Miss Milligan should join the General Pageant Committee as planner and trainer of dancing. The Pageant, which was performed at Garscube Estate in June 1928, was planned to illustrate the history of Glasgow and the West. According to the Souvenir Programme, the first episode dealing with the legend of St. Mungo was to be seen through "a rhythmically moving mass of dancing children," and it continued, "this particular use of rhythmic movement to create the atmosphere of legend is entirely new in pageantry."[11] For this "moving mass", three hundred children were recruited from all over Glasgow. Training these hordes of unknown children must have tested to the full the ingenuity and patience of even the intrepid Miss Milligan.

One of the young performers has provided a vivid pen-picture of Miss Milligan in action: "She set some music going and yelled at us to 'dance' or 'move in time'. We tried our best, but it seemed that we could do nothing to please her. . . . The week before the opening, we at last got some inkling of what was expected from us." Though not particularly enchanted by this first encounter with the intimidating Miss Milligan, the dancer of 1928 became, through time, a keen and expert member of the Scottish Country Dance Society and was, over the years of association, to become fully aware of the many sides of her personality. The writer concludes, "It was a privilege to know her, be taught by her, and recognise her high standards in country dancing. . . . She could be inspiring, irascible, charming, churlish, bouncy and bullying, but she never lowered her sights. She was, and is, unique."

It would have been surprising if Miss Milligan had omitted Scottish country dancing from the Pageant of her beloved city and it has been confirmed by several dancers that at some point they danced The Dashing White Sergeant and Glasgow Highlanders. Another interesting fact about the Glasgow Pageant of 1928 is that one of the young servant maids who watched the arrival of "Bonnie Prince Charlie" in Episode IV was Miss Muriel Gibson, the present Secretary of the RSCDS.[12]

Perhaps in preparation for the Pageant, during 1927–8, Miss Milligan attended a class in Dalcroze Eurythmics taught by a well known Glasgow pupil of Jacques Dalcroze, Miss Constance Hook, who remembers her as an eager student; "in my class she glowed with joy, moved with such spontaneity and delight that I'm sure all were inspired by her presence," she said.

It is difficult to do full justice to the sterling work done by Jean Milligan for the Scottish Country Dance Society during the first decade of its history. As teacher, examiner, adjudicator, speaker, author and director of Summer School, her efforts on behalf of the Society were unstinted and as early as April 1931, in recognition of her work, Miss Milligan was made an Honorary Life Member of the Society, the first person to be so honoured.[13] The extent of her pioneering activities is all the more remarkable when it is remembered that they had to be pursued in her spare time. As Head of Women's Physical Training at Jordanhill College, she had professional duties to fulfil and in the years 1920 to 1923, she had the additional task of inspecting physical education in schools for the Scottish Education Department.[14]

In order to keep abreast with developments in her professional field, she endeavoured to attend as many as she could of the courses arranged by the associations of physical training teachers. Miss Milligan, in fact, was a keen and active member of her professional organisations. In January 1908 the woman specialist teachers of physical training had formed the Scottish League for Organisers and Teachers of Swedish Gymnastics. Courses and conferences, many of them held at Dundas Vale and Jordanhill, were organised by the League for its members and Jean Milligan attended as a participant and as a teacher. From 1924 to 1927, she was Secretary of the League and her friend, Jane MacKay, was President. From 1929 to 1933, Miss Milligan was President. It is recognised that the Scottish League played an important part in the development of Scottish physical education and that beyond Scotland, it also made a significant impact in conjunction with the Ling Association.

The Ling Association, initially open only to Madame Österberg's students, was founded in 1899 "to place physical education on a higher basis than before." Miss Milligan joined the organisation in 1919, and possibly as a result of her influence, the Scottish League affiliated to the Ling Association in May 1923. From 1930 until 1943, she was a member of the Executive Committee of the Ling Association which, of course, necessitated regular visits to London for meetings. In the years 1923 to 1943, Miss Milligan represented the Scottish League on the Board of Advisers of the Association's *Journal of School Hygiene and Physical Education*.

Even when busy with professional organisations and their activities,

Miss Milligan never missed an opportunity of spreading the cause of Scottish country dancing. At the Holiday Course organised by the Ling Association in London in January 1923, Miss Milligan was asked "to take Scotch Dances again" and she made a similar contribution to the Holiday Courses of 1925, 1927 and 1931.[15] Furthermore, at a reunion of Dartford students at Kingsfield in 1927 "J. Milligan took dancing; large numbers entered the class, which was characterised by a great spirit of enjoyment."[16]

In these years of extensive and varied activity, Jordanhill College, inevitably, remained the central pivot of Jean Milligan's life. Teaching Scottish country dancing continued to take up much of her time there and in 1931 she was enabled to develop that aspect of her College work even further.

References

1. Winifred Holtby, *Letters to a Friend*, p. 186.
2. SCDS Annual Report 1924.
3. *RSCDS Golden Jubilee 1923–1924* (Jubilee Brochure).
4. SCDS, Minutes of Meetings of the Interim Executive Committee, Feb. 29, June 19, 1924.
5. *The Australian Women's Weekly*, Nov. 13, 1974, p. 7.
6. Jean C. Milligan, *Won't You Join the Dance*, p. 26.
7. Letter from A. Smith (Hamilton) to W. Watson (Blantyre), Jan. 25, 1802, *SCDS Bulletin*, No. 11 (March, 1932), p. 6.
8. SCDS, Minutes of Meetings of the Interim Executive Committee, June 19, 1924.
9. SCDS, Secretary's Examination Book, pp. 12, 14.
10. Jean C. Milligan, *op. cit.*, p. 113.
11. *Historical Pageant. The Story of the West* (Souvenir Programme), p. 81.
12. *Ibid.*, p. 167.
13. SCDS, Minutes of Meetings of the Executive Council, April 22, 1931.
14. Glasgow Provincial Committee for the Training of Teachers, Minutes of Meetings, Dec. 14, 1923.
15. Ling Association, Minutes of Meetings of the Executive Committee, Sept. 29, 1922, Oct. 3, 1924, Oct. 8, 1926, July 18, 1930.
16. *The Bergman Österberg Physical Training College Magazine*, No. 8 (1927), p. 299.

5   The 1930s

Whilst it is undeniable that some men, for example, Lord James Stewart, Mr. Diack and Mr. Bisset, made an invaluable contribution to the development of the Scottish Country Dance Society in its infancy, it is true, for the reasons already given, that in all the Society's activities at that time the gentlemen were vastly outnumbered by the ladies. The Glasgow Branch in the Society's Annual Report of 1931 noted that although there were more taking an interest, "the numbers

From *The New Dominie,* **December 1928.** (*By courtesy of Jordanhill College of Education*)

OUR COUNTRY DANCERS

WE DID SEE ONE MAN ON THE FLOOR

of gentlemen could be increased considerably." In a more humorous way, the same point regarding the scarcity of male country dancers was made by a cartoon which appeared in the Jordanhill College magazine, *The New Dominie*, in 1928.[1] An opportunity to remedy this situation was given to Miss Milligan in 1931 and, with characteristic enthusiasm, she seized upon this chance to bring more men into country dancing.

From the beginning of the session 1931–2 all the male students in Scotland, training as specialist teachers of physical education, were transferred to the newly opened "Scottish School of Physical Education and Hygiene" at Jordanhill College; up to this point they had been trained with their female colleagues at Dunfermline College in Fife. The Administrative Head of the Scottish School was Dr. Alister MacKenzie, Principal of Dunfermline College until 1931. At the time of transfer, it was also decided that the two year diploma course for men would be extended to three to bring it into line with the women's training course. Miss Milligan immediately proposed the inclusion of Scottish country dancing in the extended course. In deciding to accept the proposal, it is possible that Dr. MacKenzie was influenced not only by her persuasive argument but also by another member of his staff who had transferred with him from Dunfermline; this was Mr. Frank Punchard, who later became Head of the Scottish School and who at this time was an active member of the Scottish Country Dance Society. A member of that first group of third year students recalls with gratitude the intensive course in country dancing which he and his colleagues received from Miss Milligan. He says:

> We were exceedingly grateful to Miss Milligan for all the work and extra coaching she personally gave us, and at the end of our year at Jordanhill, I was deputed to hand over to her a small token of our appreciation which took the form of a small clock. I feel very proud and privileged to have been a member of that first third year course of P.E. men whom Jean Milligan helped and inspired so much and left us with a lifelong interest in Scottish country dancing.

These sentiments, expressed by one of the first of "Miss Milligan's boys", are typical of the comments offered by many others who passed through her classes in succeeding years. Miss Milligan virtually monopolised the country dancing for the P.E. men from 1931 until her retirement in 1948. The students who experienced her teaching of skip change of step, pas de basque and reels of three, often explained with the aid of blackboard and chalk, can be numbered in hundreds. Just as numerous are the stories they tell. One pre-World War student, being totally uninterested in country dancing and having absented himself from the first session, remembers being sought out by Miss Milligan in the student Common Room and firmly returned to the gym; from that

A group of staff and students of Jordanhill Training College, 1931–2. Middle row centre: Miss Milligan. Front row: students of the Scottish School of Physical Education. (*Picture by courtesy of Jordanhill College of Education*)

point he became a "wildly enthusiastic" country dancer. Recalled by a post-war student is Miss Milligan's class discipline:

> Miss Milligan stood no nonsense from this class of brash young P.E. students. She taught manners and decorum and woe betide you if you got on the wrong side of her tongue. While no light weight, she could demonstrate step technique wonderfully well and was amazingly light on her feet. Her teaching of pas de basque and skip change of step stuck so well that it was easy to pass this on when teaching oneself.

It was Miss Milligan's skilful teaching and infectious enthusiasm which most impressed the P.E. men. An Arab student, who attended the Scottish School during 1934 to 1937, remarked to one of his Scottish student contemporaries, whom he met again during the war in the Middle East, "You know, I didn't think it possible for me ever to learn your Scottish country dances – Miss Milligan proved me wrong!"

If the P.E. students never forgot Miss Milligan, she likewise never forgot them. Having a phenomenal memory for faces and names, she would recognise and often name them when they met in later years, while she was travelling in and beyond Scotland on Country Dance Society business. Her opening remarks at such reunions, however, could be devastatingly frank, as is shown by a former student to whom she said, "For one of my boys, your feet are dreadful. You'd never know I had ever taught you."

Miss Milligan is remembered with particular affection and respect by those P.E. students whom she selected to dance in her demonstration teams. Partnered by Jordanhill women students, or by dancers from the Glasgow Branch of the Society, they danced at College Sports and Gala Days. Often chauffeured by Miss Milligan herself, they also ventured further afield assisting her in the promotion of Scottish country dancing. At Church meetings, garden fêtes and occasionally in the grander setting of a "Thé Dansant", the teams demonstrated the country dances and one or two of the boys danced the Highland Fling and the Sword Dance which they had been taught by Miss Milligan in her College classes. Although there were many such demonstrations in the 30s and 40s, one or two stand out as highlights for the students who took part in them.

A large International Folk Dance Festival was held in London in July 1935 and the Scottish Country Dance Society was given an excellent opportunity for propaganda when it was invited to send a team of no fewer than fifty dancers to take part in a performance in the

Miss Milligan's "girls and boys", Jordanhill, 1936. Men (left to right): Michael Miller, George Hastie, Ford Spence, Bowman Lindsay, Bill Murray. Ladies (left to right): Miss Milligan, Mary Findlay, Nenna Murray, Jess Bisset, Bunty Stewart.

Albert Hall. When explaining to a *Weekly Herald* reporter the arrangements for the Festival, Miss Milligan was able to make the proud boast that fourteen of the men travelling south would be students of the Scottish School of Physical Education at Jordanhill.[2] It was agreed that the Society would meet part of the cost of the London visit and donations were requested from branches. Under the able leadership of Miss Milligan, the Glasgow Committee arranged a concert in the Lyric Theatre – an "All-Scottish Night" of song, verse and dance. It was so successful that the Branch was able to send a donation of £50.[3] No doubt there was further evidence of Miss Milligan's fund raising talents at the Jordanhill College Garden Fête on Saturday, 15th June 1935, when part of the proceeds was to help defray the expenses of the students representing the Country Dance Society at the Festival.[4] The Society actually sustained a loss of almost £50 but because of the success of the Scottish appearance at the Albert Hall and the propaganda benefits gained thereby, the London visit was considered to have been very worthwhile.[5]

Concerned about the state of the nation's health, early in 1937, the British government established the National Fitness Council. Its object was to improve the health of the young, particularly by training leaders for youth work and, to that end, regional committees were set

Miss Milligan's team at the National Fitness Council's Pavilion, Empire Exhibition, Glasgow, 1938.

up. Jean Milligan became a member of the Glasgow and South West Committee of the Fitness Council in September 1937 and was in consequence given another avenue for the extension of the work of the Scottish Country Dance Society.[6] The Council featured very prominently in Glasgow's Empire Exhibition of May to September 1938 and the Glasgow Branch was asked to provide teams of country dancers. The Executive Council of the Society agreed that other branches should be asked to help Glasgow and Miss M. W. Kenyon, Secretary of the Glasgow Branch, was invited to make all the necessary arrangements.[7]

Sixteen couples from Jordanhill, under Miss Milligan's direction, danced at the inaugural National Fitness Display and Concert in the Kelvin Hall, Glasgow. At the rehearsal for this event some youthful onlookers began by making fun of the dancers but were soon reduced to silence and one was heard to say, "My! that's guid! They men can dance!"[8] Miss Milligan's teams danced at the opening and closing Exhibition Balls and at the Exhibition site in Bellahouston Park. They gave several performances in May at the Clachan, the recreated Highland village, and in June and September at the National Fitness Council Pavilion.[9] Looking back on the Empire Exhibition, a Jordanhill student remembers "the atrocious weather and a platform the size of a postage stamp." In August 1938 the Society's Executive Council received good reports from Miss Milligan and Miss Kenyon of the performances by the various teams, which, it was said, had given the Society excellent publicity at the Empire Exhibition.[10]

Despite growing tension and the gathering war clouds, the next year also had pleasant memories for some of Miss Milligan's boys. In that year a Lingiad, a gymnastic festival, was held in Sweden and taking part were gymnasts from Jordanhill and Dunfermline Colleges. The Lingiad was to be followed immediately by an International Folk Dance Festival in Stockholm and the Society was very keen to accept an invitation to participate. The problem, however, was the cost. The solution, no doubt proposed by Miss Milligan, was approved by the Society's Executive Council in April 1939; the country dancers would all be included in the gymnastic teams present at the Lingiad.[11] A team of eight men from Jordanhill and eight women from Dunfermline was selected and Miss Milligan conducted the practices in preparation for the Swedish Festival. She did not travel with the dancers but later stated that she was very satisfied with the reports she had received about their dancing. Dr. McLaren from Edinburgh, who at the Society's expense accompanied the team as the Highland dancer, writing to express his gratitude said, "In my opinion the Scottish country dance team was one of the few teams who really appeared to be enjoying their dancing and it was a pleasure to watch them."[12]

There was no doubt that Miss Milligan's "conversion" of the P.E.

Some Jordanhill dancers at the International Folk Dance Festival, Stockholm, August 1939. Left to right: James Moncur, James Rae, Dixon Bennet, Dr. MacLaren (Edinburgh).

men had very significant implications for the progress and development of the Scottish country dance movement within and without Scotland. The immediate impact at Jordanhill itself is evident from the following humorous insertion in the College magazine in December 1932:

> Hitherto we had believed that we did not country dance, but we do, we do! The classes in this branch of the art, held in the gymnasia on Fridays, have grown outstandingly popular. There was almost a break-in on Friday before the SRC dance when the class was declared off.[13]

The long-term effects were of greater importance. At Jordanhill and also at Dunfermline College, for many years the Society's Preliminary Test Certificate at least was a compulsory element in teacher training for physical education; it is to be regretted that the broadening of the P.E. curriculum in recent years has made this no longer possible. Equipped with a good grounding in the basics of country dancing and with a knowledge of the standards required by the Scottish Country Dance Society, the physical education specialists were able to put this expertise to good use in their schools. The result was more teaching of country dancing in secondary, as well as primary schools, during the

1930s and 1940s. The interest developed in schools spilled over into the continuation classes for Scottish country dancing, which enjoyed great popularity in the post-war years.

Inevitably, the Country Dance Society benefited from these developments in schools and further education classes. Its membership expanded and men began to join in increasing numbers. The growing strength of the Society is reflected in the thirty-two new branches formed between 1930 and 1950. The Society benefited directly in another way from Jean Milligan's work with the P.E. students at Jordanhill. Many of her boys not only kept up their interest in country dancing in their professional work but, inspired by her zeal and dedication, also became enthusiastic members of the Scottish Country Dance Society and have continued in many capacities to promote its ideals at branch, national and international levels.

Miss Milligan's boundless energy and great vitality never failed to astonish those who knew her. Her enthusiasm for her professional work and for the Country Dance Society and its Glasgow Branch did not curtail her involvement with good causes. The late 1920s and early 1930s were years of dire unemployment and poverty; those were the days of the "Dole" and the "Hunger Marches." Miss Milligan was determined to do what she could to alleviate the distress. In 1929, the Glasgow Branch organised a dance in the Locarno Ballroom and raised £50 for the Lord Provost's Unemployment Fund.[14] Another of Miss Milligan's charitable interests was The League of Mercy, which, before the days of the National Health Service, existed for the purpose of aiding voluntary hospitals. As early as 1928, and again in 1934, Miss Milligan was invited by Lord and Lady Belhaven to assist at a Fête at Wishaw House in aid of the League. She was in charge of the sideshows, which were staffed by her Jordanhill assistants, and described on the programme as "all the fun of the fair".

One of the most depressed areas in Scotland was around Bellshill in Lanarkshire. It was there in 1932 that the Pilgrim Trust established the settlement known as Harkness House with money donated by the American banker philanthropist, Edward Stephen Harkness. As the aim of such centres was not merely to teach new skills but to widen the horizons of the unemployed through music, art, drama and dancing, the first Warden of Harkness House invited Miss Milligan to run a course in Scottish country dancing. Miss Milligan was very happy to accept the invitation and like the rest of the Harkness House staff, among them several unemployed graduate teachers, gave her services free. Her classes in games and dancing were very successful as is evident from the following commentary in a local newspaper:

Miss Milligan, we believe, is one of the most energetic women of her age, and the lively, enthusiastic way she illustrated the dancing and games was an inspiration to all students. If she were an M.P. or Head of Government, we imagine things would have to get a move on or she would know the reason why. As it is, we have her putting all the "go" of her brimming energy into teaching the lads and lasses of Harkness House how to enjoy their abundant "leisure time" – and play the game![15]

Unfortunately, Harkness House closed in 1937 and at the end of her farewell Scottish country dance lesson, Miss Milligan said that she had "scarcely deplored anything so much as the closing of Harkness House, but hoped the members would continue the good work, as they were now dancing so well."

Miss Milligan's involvement with the campaign of the National Fitness Council has already been mentioned. Three years before that campaign, in 1934, the Glasgow Keep Fit Movement was founded. Prominent amongst its founders was Miss Katherine G. Smith, one of Miss Milligan's assistants at Jordanhill. Under inspired leadership, the work of this organisation flourished not only in the city but throughout the west of Scotland, and an interesting link was immediately formed between it and the Scottish Country Dance Society. Mrs. May Brown, appointed in 1935 as Organiser of GKFM, as it was known, became Secretary of the Country Dance Society in the following year. Miss Muriel Hadden, who succeeded Mrs. Brown as Secretary of the Society in 1942 and remained in that post until 1967, was also one of the early members of the Glasgow Keep Fit Movement.

It was natural that Miss Milligan should be attracted to GKFM. She joined the Committee in December 1937 and in October 1938, she served on a sub-committee formed to discuss the setting up of a national Keep Fit organisation; the Scottish Women's Keep Fit Association was founded in December 1938. As a member of the Glasgow and South West Committee of the National Fitness Council, Miss Milligan had been working towards the procuring of a grant for the Keep Fit Movement. She was successful in her efforts and a grant was received in May 1939.[16]

References

1. *The New Dominie*, Dec., 1928, p. 13.
2. RSCDS Log, Vol. 1.
3. *SCDS Bulletin*, No. 8 (Oct., 1935), p. 7.
4. RSCDS Log, Vol. 1.
5. SCDS, Minutes of Meetings of the Publications Committee, Nov. 9, 1935.
6. Glasgow Keep Fit Movement, Minutes of Meetings, Sept., 1937.
7. SCDS, Minutes of Meetings of the Executive Council, March 19, 1938.
8. *SCDS Bulletin*, No. 13 (March, 1938), p. 9.

9. *Ibid.*, No. 14 (Oct., 1938), pp. 17–19.
10. SCDS, Minutes of Meetings of the Executive Council, Aug. 5, 1938.
11. SCDS, Minutes of Meetings of the Publications Committee, April 29, 1939.
12. *Ibid.*, Nov. 4, 1939.
13. *The New Dominie*, Dec., 1932, p. 6.
14. SCDS Annual Report 1929.
15. *Motherwell Times*, Oct. 21, 1932.
16. Glasgow Keep Fit Movement, Minutes of Meetings: Sept., Oct., Dec., 1937; May, 1939.

6   The War Years

Despite the lowering clouds of war, the Summer School of the Scottish Country Dance Society took place as usual at St. Andrews in August 1939, with greater numbers than ever before. The usual activities, classes, social dancing, the Younger Hall dances and Mr. Reid's Highland classes continued with unabated vigour. That last pre-war Summer School was blessed with beautiful weather and members sunbathed on the beach, trying not to listen to the constant overhead manoeuvres of RAF planes from Leuchars.

Shortly after this, came the outbreak of war. With their classes for the session 1939–40 already planned, many branches were faced with a problem. Not only were some schools and public halls requisitioned by the government but very few indeed had sufficient blackout to satisfy air raid precautions. The branches struggled as best they could to cope with these difficulties; it was noted in November 1939 that in some places – Glasgow, Hamilton, Lanark, North Ayrshire and Arbroath – a good start had been made.[1] All the "lets" of Glasgow schools were cancelled but the Branch had a class in a Lanarkshire school. As this was in a "neutral" area, the let was granted but the class had to meet on a Saturday afternoon because the school had no blackout. In the city of Glasgow itself, the problem was partly solved by the management of Green's Playhouse, which gave the Branch the use of the ballroom for two classes. Miss Milligan's Tuesday class met at its usual time, 5.30–7.00 p.m. and was largely composed of teachers, though many faithful members could not attend, having been evacuated with their schools away from the city. The class enjoyed to the full the undiminished enthusiasm of Miss Milligan's teaching and the superb music provided by Miss Jenny Waddell. One advantage of the early start was that, except from November to January, the class began in the dim twilight before complete blackout; by seven o'clock when the class finished, if there were no moon, torches were necessary for the journey home. Miss Milligan's "Circle", a country dance class popular with the Glasgow medical profession, also "went on merrily" despite the war.

When halls became more available, branches were able to run classes, if not weekly, as regularly as possible. Classes were inevitably small and some branches were obliged to meet the resulting deficit from their funds. Many teachers and pianists gave their services free. At one Glasgow Branch class, the teacher collected such fees as came in, paid for the let of the school, recompensed the janitor and shared the balance with the pianist. Inspired by the example of Miss Milligan, teacher and pianist were entirely satisfied.

In addition to guiding her own Branch through its wartime difficulties, Miss Milligan continued as before to work on behalf of the Society in places furth of Glasgow. As a member of the Publications Committee, she was closely associated with the Society's determined efforts to survive the war. The *Scottish Country Dance Society Bulletin* of October 1940 said:

> At a time when there is so much destruction and horror in the world, it is surely a duty of a Society such as ours to keep alive dances and music which bring gaiety and happiness to so many.[2]

The Executive Council met only once during the war on 16th November 1940 and did not meet again until 2nd August 1945. In the interval, Society business was conducted by the Publications Committee, which from May 1942 was called the Management Committee. There were financial worries caused by the fall in subscriptions but there were also developments which gave great encouragement to the Management Committee. According to the *Bulletin* of November 1941, Scottish country dancing continued in schools, camps, youth centres, evening classes and ARP posts. The *War Economy Bulletin* of June 1942, a single sheet, reported Scottish country dance courses in England taught by Mrs. Brown, Miss Webster and Miss Milligan and noted that many classes were being taught by Jordanhill men to overseas troops as well as to Scottish regiments. In Edinburgh, too, Miss Anderson and Mrs. Lesslie conducted very successful weekly classes for the Scottish Command.[3]

There can be no greater tribute to the teaching and inspiration of Miss Milligan than that demonstrated by those Jordanhill students who, during the war, shared their country dance knowledge with their colleagues in the Forces. From a letter sent to Miss Milligan, here is an extract which exemplifies their loyalty and dedication:

> In the midst of the strife of war, I have been asked to start a country dancing class in the Battalion, and my books (yes, I had them) repose in some ditch in France. Could you out of the kindness of your heart send me what literature you consider necessary for beginners – steps, simple dances etc. . . . . I shall be glad also of news of your classes and your "team", and your many activities in connection with the Association. . . .[4]

The popularity of Scottish country dancing with the Forces was very encouraging but particularly gratifying were the reports that the country dance was also serving to relieve the tedium of imprisonment in POW camps. Mrs. Harris Hunter, Secretary of the Perth Branch, informed Headquarters that her husband, Lt.-Col. T. Harris Hunter,

51st Division, RASC, had started a country dance class in Oflag VIIC/H, Germany, where he was a prisoner and where a new dance had been invented. This was The Reel of the 51st Division, known originally as The St. Valery Reel, which became the first non-traditional dance to be adopted and published by the Society. At her husband's request, Mrs. Harris Hunter sent off one of the Society's books and hoped that it would reach him.[5] In 1944 the Glasgow Branch responded to an appeal for country dance books from prisoners in Stalag 344.[6]

The popularity of country dancing at home inevitably meant an increasing demand for teachers and, throughout the war, there were regular examinations for the Society's teaching certificate. One particular examination, in the summer of 1940, demonstrates the spirit of dedication and determination which characterised country dancers at this time; it was an examination arranged by Miss Milligan in a Glasgow class for Miss Nan Shaw of Belfast. In order to visit Scotland, Miss Shaw had to obtain a travel permit and was obliged, for security reasons, to carry her country dance books in an official envelope complete with large blobs of sealing wax. The difficult journey was not in vain, for the examination was successful and Miss Shaw was charged by Miss Milligan "to go back and keep teaching," which, of course, she did.

Undeterred by the familiar slogan, "Is your journey really necessary?" and by the uncomfortable conditions on packed and unheated trains, Miss Milligan, as adjudicator, teacher and examiner, continued to travel on behalf of the Country Dance Society. In July 1942 she held a week's course in Rochdale for thirty teachers who were released from their schools so that they might benefit from her instruction. The enthusiasm generated by Miss Milligan, amongst the teachers, resulted in the formation of the Rochdale Branch early in 1943.[7]

With her cheerful and enthusiastic disposition, Miss Milligan must have been very welcome wherever she went. In 1943, Manchester Branch requested "a visit from Headquarters in order to encourage members and give them a fillip." The task was assigned to Miss Milligan who, during the morning and afternoon of Saturday, 24th July, held classes in Broughton High School, Manchester. She gave her services free and of her classes, it was said that they were "thoroughly successful" and that "everyone seemed to feel the urge to dance well."[8]

The annual Summer School at St. Andrews, planned for 1940, had had to be cancelled and it was not possible to arrange another until 1945. To some extent, the one day courses taught by Miss Milligan and other Society teachers compensated for this lack. The Glasgow Branch held such courses at Jordanhill College, where morning classes were followed by lunch and a dance which, owing to blackout restrictions, had to be held in the afternoon. The seventy to eighty dancers were guided and directed by Miss Milligan, "who made everyone feel that they had been transported to the happy atmosphere of a St. Andrews social evening." In January and December 1944, the Society organised two very successful weekend courses in Edinburgh, at which the teachers were Miss Anderson of Edinburgh and Miss Milligan.

From the beginning of the war, Miss Milligan had once again shown her determination to undertake patriotic work in a wide variety of ways. At the Forces canteen in Glasgow Central Station, she worked regularly, sometimes in the steamy atmosphere of the kitchen, at other times, less tiringly, as cashier. Her previous training in VAD work she put to good use as a member of the First Aid Post near her Glasgow home at 22 Roxburgh Street. A characteristic incident, in 1943, is shown by the following newspaper account:

On the first night of the Glasgow blitz the inhabitants of No. 22 stumbled down to the cellar, variously arrayed, and carrying torches and small attache cases. In an atmosphere of nervous gloom they struggled with deck chairs and swathed themselves in rugs. And then there was the firm patter of another pair of feet on the cellar stairs, and in the doorway appeared a small, rotund figure clad in a brown fur coat.

The coat was surmounted by a round, cheerful face. Above that again was a tea cosy, with an enamel basin on top, the whole kept in place with a wool scarf tied under the chin. Miss Jean Milligan, member of the local First Aid Post was not to be discomfited by the temporary shortage of steel helmets.

There was a gust of fear-dispelling laughter and in a moment or two the company were snugly seated round the little stove, sucking barley sugar. "Good for the nerves," said Miss Jean, proferring a glass jar and ready to face whatever the night might bring.[9]

In this wartime recollection, those who knew Miss Milligan will no doubt recognise two of her outstanding characteristics – an enviable lack of self-consciousness and the ability to instil her own cheerful spirit into those around her.

Always a devotee of "good causes", Miss Milligan found an abundance of outlets for her active interest during the war. Her friend Miss Jane MacKay, then living in Largs, was closely associated with the work of the Navy League which provided comforts such as warm clothing, books and magazines for the sailors of the Royal Navy. Miss Milligan set about raising funds for the League by inspiring many Branch and Society members to contribute the proceeds of any social activities they were able to organise. The indefatigable and expert knitter also got down to work with needles and wool, and so, of course, did her country dance disciples. One Glasgow class member, less expert than the teacher, handed over an exceedingly outsize navy blue wool sweater with the timid remark, "I'm afraid this would fit Goliath." "Never mind, sailors are big men," was the consoling reply as Miss Milligan swept it into her equally capacious bag.

She was the driving force behind many charitable events in Glasgow. Early in 1941 the Branch, in co-operation with the Glasgow Branch of the English Folk Dance and Song Society, arranged an "International Night" at which Poles, Austrians and Indians, as well as the local dancers, gave demonstrations of their national dances. The event attracted about 300 people and the money raised was sent to the International War Fund.[10] A good cause, very dear to Miss Milligan's heart, was the "51st Division Comforts Fund", suggested by a Glasgow Branch member after learning The Reel of the 51st Division. Administered by Headquarters, the Fund received almost £170 in donations from branches. On assurances that they could send gifts to imprisoned members of the 51st Division, the money was divided between the Red Cross Centres of Elgin, Perth and Rothesay for the purchase of chanters, bagpipes, music, records, books, footballs and games.[11]

In 1940, having closed down the National Fitness Council before the outbreak of war, the government once again became concerned about the physical and moral welfare of Britain's young people. A government sponsored movement was set up. At first known as the "Youth Emergency Service", its main purpose was the provision of youth clubs throughout the country. Here again the expertise of the Scottish Country Dance Society and the educational and recreational value of its work was recognised. At a meeting organised by the Ministry of Labour to form a committee to deal with various forms of recreative facilities for youth Miss Anderson of Edinburgh represented the Society. As the intention was to promote all-round development, physical activities and games played a large part in club programmes, thus creating a need for suitably qualified leaders, especially for country dancing, which soon became one of the most popular pastimes. At first, unfortunately, the quality of teaching was poor and early in 1941, the Society took action to remedy this. The Secretary, Mrs. Brown, had an interview with Dr. Jardine, Secretary of the Scottish Education Department and he promised to look into the matter.[12] Thereafter, many Education Committees organised training courses for leaders and awarded certificates but Miss Milligan was still not satisfied with the standard of teaching achieved. She was determined that Education Committees should insist on the Society's certificates as a qualification for teaching Scottish country dancing in youth clubs. First Lanarkshire, then Glasgow and later other

Committees, were eventually persuaded by her sheer persistence to agree to this. In this way, Miss Milligan was able to ensure the maintenance of standards set by the Country Dance Society.

Miss Milligan's involvement in youth work was not confined to training and examining teachers; she took a personal interest in many club members, one of whom has provided an example of her thoughtfulness. The young woman was awarded her Scottish country dance certificates by Miss Milligan and was also successful in gaining a Keep-Fit Leader's certificate. On learning that the newly certificated teacher of country dancing was to be "called up" for munitions work, Miss Milligan, considering this a waste, was prepared to intervene in order to ensure that her qualifications in physical activities were put to better use in one of the Services. Although, in fact, she was not called up either for munitions or into the Services and was able to teach keep-fit and country dancing during the war, the young woman was always grateful for Miss Milligan's concerned interest in her.

Throughout these years of war, while tirelessly fulfilling her Country Dance Society duties in Glasgow and elsewhere, Miss Milligan's work as Head of Women's Physical Education at Jordanhill continued during College sessions and at vacation courses. One such course, which she taught for several years, was entitled "Play Centres and Physical Activities for Children". These activities consisted chiefly of singing games, simple team games, a little mime and some occasional items based on Dalcroze Eurhythmics. One member of the course in 1944 says that the class welcomed the supply of new ideas and, at a time when rubber balls were unobtainable, equally welcome were the *ersatz* balls made during the course from old silk stockings and ripped out wool.

At the College, Miss Milligan and her assistant, Miss Smith, established a branch of the National Savings Association and through their efforts, a great deal of money was raised. Miss Milligan's casual method of collecting the money, "pushing it into different pockets as she went about her College business," did cause some concern, not always allayed by her airy assurance that "it would all work out." That it did so, was attributed to her marvellous memory for faces and names. Silver paper collection was another wartime activity which involved Miss Milligan and the College P.E. staff.

As already indicated in an earlier chapter, from long before the war until well after it, one of Miss Milligan's most cherished College projects was the annual Gala Day. These continued during the war and a number of charities, including the Thistle Foundation for the War Blinded, benefited from them. The 1943 summer issue of the student magazine, *The New Dominie*, promised its readers "A Gala Day on 18th June; dancing on the green, drama and a boost for the war effort."

Gala Day, Jordanhill Training College, June 1945. Foreground (left to right): Audrey Muir and Duncan McSwein, Peggy McMaster and Graeme Stephens, May Alexander and William J. Ireland, Mary Thompson and John M. Mitchell.

In the autumn of 1944, as the war at last began to draw to a close, there was a marked upsurge of interest in Scottish country dancing. People who had sacrificed their enjoyment of dancing to concentrate on the war effort now found themselves with fewer demands on their time and energy and able to return to their classes. An entry in the diary of a Glasgow Branch member reads as follows:

October 24. This was the first night of Miss Milligan's class. Both the Beginners' and Advanced classes are huge, thanks to the relaxation of the Blackout and Fire Guard duties. Sometimes I wonder at the seeming temerity of the Government in releasing us from these duties and restrictions. The war must be more nearly over than we know.

In keeping with this same mood of optimism, the Management Committee of the Society, in February 1945, began to make arrangements for a Summer School at St. Andrews and unanimously invited Miss Milligan to be the Director. When the School met in August, the conflict in the Far East still continued and, true to her constant interest in national affairs, Miss Milligan gathered the members together to hear, on the radio, the official announcement of what came to be known as VJ Day. It was a solemn occasion. Otherwise it was a very happy Summer School. The weather was excellent and there was a surprising abundance of food in University Hall, where, despite strict rationing, the staff still made sure that the dancers were well fed. At an overflowing morning class, Miss Milligan taught Book 13, the "Victory Book" which, of course, included The Reel of the 51st Division.

Though, reluctantly, she did eventually change her point of view, newly devised dances were not favoured by Miss Milligan at this time. The Reel of the 51st Division, clearly, was an exception because of its background history and because in 1944 Her Majesty the Queen had expressed the hope that "it would be published some day."[13]

Now that branches were able to return to and in some cases even exceed the level of pre-war activities, Miss Milligan's presence at their functions was being requested more and more. Easier travel made it possible for her to accept these invitations and not just for Scotland and England, because in 1947 she made her first "overseas" trip to visit the Belfast Branch. In July 1946 she travelled to London with sixty-six dancers who took part in an International Youth Festival at Wembley, organised by the Central Council of Physical Recreation. A dancer present at that event has described an incident which confirms that Miss Milligan had emerged from the war years with her vitality and resourcefulness quite undiminished. The distance in the arena between the dancers and the band of the Scots Guards resulted in a chaotic start to the Scottish performance. True to form, and undaunted by an audience of about 40,000, Miss Milligan marched into the arena, shouted, "Stop! Stop!" and then proceeded by use of voice and arms to ensure that band and dancers began again, this time in perfect unison!

In the immediate post-war years, Miss Milligan's passionate interest in the Society, which she had created, was becoming all absorbing so she decided to use all her time and energy in its further development. After thirty-nine years of loyal service, broken only by the short spell in Malta, she retired from her post at Jordanhill Training College. Tributes to her work came from many sources. No doubt none pleased Miss Milligan more than the simply worded appreciation which appeared in the College magazine under the heading "Goodbye to Miss Milligan":

> To past and present students of the College alike, the news that Miss Milligan is leaving will be sad news indeed. Her wonderful personality and helpfulness have become part of the College which we thankfully take for granted, and we know that they can never be replaced.
>
> In her Physical Training classes, Country Dancing, Gala Day organising and the many other spheres in which we have known her, we will miss her cheery and helpful presence.
>
> She has been training teachers in Glasgow since 1909; a long time, Miss Milligan, but happy years we know. It is our sincere wish that the years to come will be even happier ones and that you will return to see us often.[14]

In fact, she kept in touch with Jordanhill until the end of her life, thirty years later, retaining her interest in and friendship with not only the staff of her own Department of Physical Education but with the whole College.

At this time of retirement, it was also appropriate that the many years of service to physical education should have been recognised by her professional colleagues. The following tribute to her was paid on behalf of the Ling Association:

"Miss Milligan – retired." These words do not somehow go together. Wherever Miss Milligan is present there life and enthusiasm are also present, and whatever happens, we cannot afford to let that depart from our profession, especially at the present moment. True, she has resigned from her post as Principal Lecturer in Physical Education at Jordanhill College after 39 years strenuous service during which latterly an average of 1,000 teachers passed through her hands each year. Her loss to the Department, to the Scottish Education Authority and to Scottish teachers generally must be inestimable, but to our Association here in England their loss may be our gain. Now that she is so-called "free-lance" and no longer tied to Scotland, maybe, who knows we shall see more of her at our Courses and perhaps be privileged again to take part in her classes. To be taught by Miss Milligan is a physical, mental and cultural experience . . . and thus we may once again enjoy the feeling of lift-poise deportment, which one associates with her teaching, together with the disciplined silence which is signalled merely by an expressive lift of the eyebrows. Enjoyment is always there, coinciding with the feeling of, and wholesome demand for, accuracy and team work.

Congratulations, Miss Milligan, on your past years and welcome to the future!

M.E.S.[15]

Without any doubt, the writer of those words would not have been surprised to learn that Miss Milligan's future was to be as busy and as productive as her past.

References

1. SCDS, Minutes of Meetings of the Publications Committee, Nov. 4, 1939.
2. *SCDS Bulletin*, No. 17 (Oct., 1940), p. 1.
3. *Ibid.*, No. 19 (Nov., 1941), p. 1; *ibid., War Economy Bulletin*, June, 1942.
4. *Ibid.*, No. 17 (Oct., 1940), p. 4.
5. *Ibid.*, No. 18 (June, 1941), p. 3.
6. *Ibid.*, No. 22 (Dec., 1944), p. 6.
7. *Ibid.*, No. 20 (Dec., 1942). p. 4.
8. SCDS, Minutes of Meetings of the Management Committee, May 22, 1943; SCDS, Manchester Branch, Minutes of Meetings, Aug. 8, 1943.
9. RSCDS Log, Vol. 1.
10. *SCDS Bulletin*, No. 19 (Nov., 1941), p. 3.
11. *Ibid.*, No. 21 (Nov., 1943).

12. SCDS, Minutes of Meetings of the Management Committee, Feb. 15, 1941.
13. *SCDS Bulletin*, No. 22 (Dec., 1944), p. 2.
14. *The New Dominie.*, Summer 1948, p. 25.
15. *The Monthly Leaflet of the Ling Association*, Vol. 49, No. 7 (Aug.–Sept., 1948), p. 145.

Travels Abroad

Nineteen forty-eight, the year of Miss Milligan's retirement, was also significant for the Scottish Country Dance Society and its Glasgow Branch. It was the year of their twenty-fifth anniversary. At a dance held at Jordanhill College in June, the first Honorary Secretary of the Glasgow Branch, Mr. R. Percy Thomson, paid tribute to Miss Milligan's tireless energy and enthusiasm throughout the previous twenty-five years. On behalf of the Branch he presented to her a wallet of notes together with a bound volume of all the books published by the Society.[1] Very appropriately, the Society's Annual General Meeting of 1948 was held in Glasgow and on that occasion the Chairman, Mrs. Hamilton Meikle, congratulated Mrs. Stewart and Miss Milligan "on the work they had done in founding the Scottish Country Dance Society twenty-five years ago, and in inspiring and developing its work." The Chairman presented each lady with a handbag and a cheque.[2]

As the Society began its second quarter century, the founders could reflect with satisfaction upon the achievements of the first. The Annual Report of October 1951 referred to the Society's "unprecedented vitality". The membership had grown to 11,500; there were 55 branches, including the first two overseas, Boston and Cape Town, and there were 118 affiliated groups scattered throughout the world.[3] At this time the principal pioneers of the 1920s were still actively concerned with the work of their Society – Lord James as President, Mrs. Stewart as Vice-President and Miss Milligan as Chairman of the Executive Council. By the end of the decade, however, that triumvirate no longer existed.

In the late 1950s Mrs. Stewart decided to make her permanent home in South Africa. It was Mrs. Stewart who first had the idea to form a Scottish Country Dance Society; to her also must go the credit for having taken the first steps towards its foundation. She was Honorary Secretary from 1923 until 1933 when she became Vice-President and, from her home in South Africa, continued to take a great interest in the Society's activities until the end of her life in 1968.[4] It was very pleasing to Mrs. Stewart that she lived long enough to see the Society, which she had inspired, grow into a flourishing world-wide movement.

Lord James, whose outstanding work in the early days of the Scottish Country Dance Society has been described in an earlier chapter, died in May 1957. Despite increasing deafness and failing

The Duke of Atholl (Lord James
Stewart Murray) President of the
Royal Scottish Country Dance
Society, 1924–57.

eyesight, he presided over Annual General Meetings right to the end
of his life. In his last presidential remarks, delivered at Dundee on 27th
October 1956, Lord James returned to one of his favourite themes and
reminded his listeners that the Society could help "to broaden the
cultural relationship between all countries."[5]

Mrs. Stewart's emigration to South Africa and the ill health and
subsequent death of Lord James inevitably meant increasing demands

on the time and energy of Miss Milligan. Already in November 1952, Lord James had informed the members present at the Annual General Meeting in Glasgow that having read the Branch Reports he was "struck by the fact that Miss Milligan seemed to have solved the secret of perpetual motion."[6] Miss Milligan was able to respond to the many requests for her skills as teacher, adjudicator and examiner because, she was now retired from Jordanhill College and also because, in 1952, she had relinquished her large commitment to the affairs of the Glasgow Branch. Apart from the early years when Mr. Michael Diack presided, she had served the Branch as President and Chairman since 1929. Although relieved of the burden of Branch business and able in consequence to give more time to the Society at large, Miss Milligan never lost her interest in the "oldest Branch". She became its Honorary President in 1952, made generous donations in cash and kind to various Branch projects and, until the year before her death, was always the principal teacher at the Glasgow Weekend Schools in the Palace of Art.

In 1948 Miss Milligan made her first trip abroad on behalf of the Society. As its delegate, she attended a Conference of the International Folk Music Council held in Basle and on her return reported that she had been invited to send a team of dancers to the Council's next Conference.[7] As a result, a Society Team, led by Miss Milligan, travelled to Venice in Sepember 1949 to participate in a Conference and Festival. This was the first of the International Teams which, during the next ten years, represented Scotland and the Society at International Folk Dance Festivals in Italy, France, Holland, Spain, Norway, South Africa and Germany. The members of the International Teams were chosen by audition. This process of selection continued until 1959 when the Executive Council decided that future invitations to international festivals would be offered to interested branches with the Society prepared to assist financially when necessary.[8]

Those dancers who were chosen to join the International Team have said how much they enjoyed the experience of acting as ambassadors for the Society and of travelling abroad with Miss Milligan. Although she was not available on every occasion, it was usually the co-founder who escorted the teams. As team leader her first concern was always for the welfare of the dancers and on one trip she was very unhappy when the accommodation provided did not match up to her expectations. A high standard of dancing was demanded from the teams and each performance was well rehearsed, although Miss Milligan steadfastly refused to succumb to the continental practice of rehearsing and performing on the Sabbath. On these trips, nevertheless, there was also a great deal of fun in which the team leader always participated. She never missed a party in the evening even after

Miss Milligan and Miss Hadden with some members of the first International Team, 1949. Ladies (left to right): Doris Robertson, Irene Grant, Miss Hadden, Miss Milligan, Margaret Moir. Gentlemen (left to right): Bill Murray, Iain Robertson, Bill Clement.

a long day of processions and demonstrations. A dancer at Nice remembers her "not with the team, but marching along in the broiling sun through the milling crowds at the sides of the road, during the long march to the War Memorial on Bastille Day." Her energy and stamina frequently astonished the dancers, as also did her ability to achieve the seemingly impossible. At Amsterdam in 1951 when given the chance to teach all the national groups present at the Festival, she soon had the large assembly enjoying Scottish country dancing. The language barrier presented no problems for Miss Milligan; "Milligan-Esperanto", a mixture of French, English, German and Dutch, combined with skilful teaching and a dominating personality, achieved the required result.[9]

Undoubtedly, these trips abroad were beneficial to the RSCDS and resulted in an increase of interest in Scotland's national dances. The Scottish teams were always well received wherever they went, their music, costume and elegant dancing ensuring a good response from their audiences. Much of their success, of course, was due to the personality of their director who, whether in conference with other

Miss Milligan with the
International Team in Bavaria,
1956.

experts in national music and dance or when present with the Scottish
team at a spectacularly grand concert, never failed to make a deep
impression upon her audience. An incident at the Bergen Festival in
1955 gives a clear indication of her popularity. The final concert of the
Festival took place in an open-air theatre; just before dancing their
farewell dance, "Rouken Glen", the members of the Scottish team
were surprised and delighted, as were the 30,000 spectators who
applauded tumultuously, when their leader was presented with a huge
bouquet of flowers in Norwegian colours.[10]

Miss Milligan loved to travel and the overseas expansion of the
Country Dance Society during the 1950s, 60s and 70s provided many
opportunities for extensive tours abroad. In 1957 she made her first
visit to North America at the invitation of Miss Jeannie Carmichael,
the founder of the Boston Branch, and of Mr. Jack McKelvie of New
Hampshire.[11] About a dozen members of the Boston Branch were
invited to meet the visitor from Scotland soon after her arrival. Two
members of that group, recalling the occasion, say that they went to
meet her "not knowing quite what to expect." "This meeting," they
continue, "was our first introduction to a very charming and gracious,
yet forceful personality, and we immediately got a liberal dose of that
enthusiasm for Scottish dancing which Miss Milligan has spread to so
many around the world."[12]

The first North American tour also included a visit to Canada. Often providing her own music at the piano, Miss Milligan taught general classes, prepared candidates for the Teacher's Certificate and conducted examinations for the Society's teaching qualifications. In this, as in later tours, the examinations were particularly important because they provided Scottish country dance groups with qualified teachers and eventually enabled those groups to achieve branch status. The Annual Report of October 1958 recorded the success of the North American tour and continued as follows:

It would be difficult for any Society to find someone more capable of inspiring people with enthusiasm for our dances and of giving them exhilaration through their performance, than the co-founder of the

Miss Milligan prepared for her last overseas trip in March 1977.

Society, Miss Jean Milligan. Her visits to America and Canada have brought numerous unsolicited testimonials from many people whom she met during her tour.[13]

The enthusiasm generated by Miss Milligan had two immediate results, namely the foundation of two Canadian branches, Toronto and Montreal, and the formation in 1958 of the Teachers' Association of Canada. Since 1967 the TAC, an association of RSCDS teachers, has been responsible for organising every other year an examination tour of North America by examiners from Britain. For the past twenty-five years, the Teachers' Association has done much to spread and to sustain those standards of teaching and dancing advocated by Miss Milligan during her first and many subsequent excursions across the Atlantic.

In later life, Miss Milligan claimed that she had visited Canada twelve times and the United States fourteen times. There can be no doubt that she enjoyed all of those visits. On her return home, she never missed an opportunity at the Summer School and elsewhere to recount her experiences and to urge the Society's members in Britain to emulate the zeal and enthusiasm of those she had met in the New World. The co-founder crossed the Atlantic for the last time in 1977 when, at the age of ninety and with two new plastic knee joints, she carried out a tour which included Montreal, Ottawa, Toronto, Hamilton, St. Catherines, Minneapolis, Winnipeg, Vancouver, Victoria, San Francisco, Los Angeles, San Diego, Honolulu, Houston, Atlanta, Washington, New York, Boston, Presque Isle, New Haven and New York. She had hoped to go from Hawaii to Japan but, she confided to a friend in Johannesburg, "I thought it would really be too much." En route home to Scotland, the indefatigable lady did manage to fit in examinations at Nottingham and Birmingham.[14]

When travelling, both at home and abroad, Miss Milligan was always a welcome house guest. She was easy to entertain and could make herself at home very quickly, especially if there were children or young people in the house and a cat on which to lavish attention. Into the "wee sma' 'oors", she would happily knit and chat, often revealing, to close friends, aspects of her character which were at variance with the public image of the confident and dominating teacher and leader. At times, for example, she indicated that she was not always sure of "herself and her doings" and said that "camouflage" was important to her in her teaching, really often putting on "an act of sureness". In old age there was her feeling of loneliness, despite a world-wide Scottish country dance family. Surprising though it is, in view of her busy life, Miss Milligan fulfilled, and very much enjoyed, the role of housekeeper in the last family home in Saltoun Street, Glasgow. Naturally, she felt very deeply the loss of her two sisters, especially

Miss Milligan in Honolulu in 1977.

Miss Milligan in party mood at Toronto, 5 April 1977. From left to right: Miss Milligan, Bill Stoddart, Frances Gray, Ruth Jappy (seated), David Grant, and at the piano Alex Jappy and Stan Hamilton.

Margaret who was her "true and willing confidante". In the homes of friends, she liked nothing better than to be allowed into the kitchen in order to repay the hospitality she had received by making her tablet, girdle scones or "Scotch" pancakes.

Miss Milligan relaxing with a favourite pastime and a favourite animal.

In 1974 the co-founder achieved her wish to meet those of the "family", as she now liked to describe the Royal Scottish Country Dance Society, who lived in the antipodes. A visit of more than three weeks to New Zealand was followed immediately by tours of Australia and South Africa. Miss Milligan loved it all. Here is an extract from her own account of the trip:

> While I enjoyed every visit I think the most thrilling was my visit to New Zealand. I was the first official visitor from the Society to the furthest off part of the world. What a wild dream such a visit would have been to me in 1923 when our thoughts of arousing interest in our dances did not go further than Scotland. What a wonderful reception I got! Practically a stranger from the North to the very South. I felt like a queen and made so many friends whom I shall never forget.[15]

Throughout the tour there were the usual hectic programmes of teaching and examining, interspersed with sight-seeing and interviews on radio, television and by the press. In those interviews, Miss Milligan was delighted to speak at length about the love of her life, Scottish country dancing, and on occasions took the chance to pass on some of her long-held beliefs. A Canberra interviewer, for example, learnt about the efficacy of a wad of blotting paper applied to the chest

August 1974. Reunited in New Zealand with Mrs. Florence Lesslie, formerly of Edinburgh and Chairman of the Royal Scottish Country Dance Society from 1955 to 1958.

as a preventative of travel sickness by land, sea and air. "It's very old, but there's a lot of truth in it," she said, adding, "For double effect, sit on newspaper."[16] There was one matter, however, about which she would allow no discussion – her age; all attempts to establish her exact years were firmly resisted. To a Christchurch reporter she said, "I am getting old and I am getting lame, but in my heart I am full of dancing."[17]

The lameness mentioned by Miss Milligan was the result of osteo-arthritis which with advancing years was causing her increasing pain. Though otherwise very fit physically, this ailment had troubled her for several years and she was therefore delighted to hear of the operation which replaced faulty joints and knee-caps with plastic substitutes. The operation on her first leg was performed in December 1975; normally six months should elapse before the second operation but Miss Milligan insisted on undergoing it eight weeks later. She actually taught at the Glasgow Weekend School a few days before the first operation and, after the second, directed the selection of staff and students for the St. Andrews Summer School from her hospital bed.

Miss Milligan was immensely proud of her "brand new knees" and was deeply grateful to her surgeon. Determined not only to walk but to dance again, she worked indefatigably towards that goal. On one occasion she called a taxi for Queen Street Railway Station, simply to test her ability to get in and out of the vehicle unaided. Having arrived at the station, she told an astonished ticket collector, "I've no ticket and I'm not travelling, but I'd like to see if I can get into and out of a train."

Such was the impression made on the Scottish country dance family by Miss Milligan's courage and determination before and after the operations that, in 1977, it was decided to nominate her as a candidate for the International Award for Valour in Sport. This is presented annually by the London Victoria Sporting Club to sportsmen and women who have bravely faced and overcome their injuries. The letter from the RSCDS Secretary accompanying the nomination stated: "Miss Milligan's fortitude and undoubted courage in undergoing two major operations for the sake of continuing her life's work merits some recognition." Though the award finally went to Niki Lauda, the Austrian racing driver, every Society member was glad that their indomitable co-founder had been selected as one of six finalists.

Pursuit of that life's work involved Miss Milligan in world-wide travel frequently during her last thirty years. Though these excursions took up an increasing amount of her time, she nevertheless continued to play a leading role in the affairs of the Society at home. She was Director of the annual Summer School and from 1945 until 1961 she served the Society continuously in the offices of Chairman and Vice-Chairman of the Executive Council. In 1957 she declined the

Presidency on the death of the Duke of Atholl but in 1961 she accepted election to the Vice-Presidency.[18] During these years Miss Milligan was associated with a number of important developments for the Scottish Country Dance Society.

Always a great admirer of the Royal Family, the co-founder must have been especially delighted when, in 1951, King George VI gave his gracious permission for the Society to use the word "Royal" in its title. This was not the first instance of royal interest in and approval of the Country Dance Society. At Holyrood House in 1944 Mrs. Stewart, Mrs. Hamilton Meikle, the Chairman, and Miss Hadden, the Secretary, presented bound copies of the Society's Books 1 to 12 to the Queen and to Princess Elizabeth, both of whom expressed appreciation of the Society's work.[19] In 1946 a team from the Edinburgh Branch was invited to demonstrate country dances before the Royal family in the forecourt of Holyrood House, the first of many such demonstrations.[20] Princess Elizabeth became the Society's

Assisted by Mr. J. Taylor and Mr. W. Little, Miss Milligan trying out the "new knees" in the Younger Hall, St. Andrews, July 1976. Miss Kitty McLauchlan is at the piano.

Miss Muriel F. Hadden,
Secretary of the Royal Scottish
Country Dance Society, 1942–67.

Patron in 1946 and when she married in 1948, Miss Anderson and Mrs. Lesslie of the Edinburgh Branch composed the dance "The Duke and Duchess of Edinburgh" to mark the occasion. On her accession in 1952, Queen Elizabeth graciously consented to continue royal patronage of the Society and in 1953, during the Coronation State Visit to Scotland, Miss Milligan, as Chairman and co-founder, was presented to the royal couple after a massed demonstration of country dances at the International Rugby Ground, Murrayfield, Edinburgh.[21]

The Annual Report of October 1955 records another important stage in the progress of the Royal Scottish Country Dance Society. In that year, premises at 12 Coates Crescent, Edinburgh, were purchased in order to set up permanent headquarters befitting an organisation with royal patronage and ever-expanding activities.[22] The property in the New Town of Edinburgh was acquired entirely through the efforts of the Society, which, as the co-founder often boasted, had never requested nor received public money. Miss Milligan made a persuasive and successful appeal to members to assist by donation with items of furniture. The inauguration of the new offices was carried out by the Secretary, Miss Muriel Hadden. Miss Hadden had been Secretary since 1942, although she had been assisting her predecessor, Mrs. May Brown, for several years before that. Her Secretaryship spanned years of significant growth for the Society. Miss Hadden's patient helpfulness was a continual source of encouragement not just to those who met her at Headquarters and at Summer School but also to members who knew her only as a considerate and reliable correspondent. When, to the great regret of all, Miss Hadden decided to retire in 1967, Miss Milligan paid tribute to her as follows:

> Miss Hadden was loved by many and admired and respected by all known and unknown to her. Those who knew her personally recognised her sterling qualities; her dignity and poise on all occasions; her kindness and help to any who needed it and her enthusiasm and interest in everything to do with Scottish country dancing and Scottish country dancers.[23]

In view of her long and dedicated service, it was fortunate and very appropriate that Miss Hadden, six years prior to her retirement, was able to take part with Miss Milligan in another outstanding event in the Society's history. On 28th June 1961, Lady Elgin, the President, accompanied by Miss Milligan, Miss Hadden and a number of specially invited representatives from Britain and overseas, welcomed the Queen and the Duke of Edinburgh to Headquarters. During their visit, the royal couple admired the recently completed portrait of Miss Milligan by the artist H. Raeburn Dobson and showed great interest in the maps which were displayed to indicate the geographical spread of the Society's 88 branches and 196 affiliated groups.[24] Observant onlookers noted that when the moment arrived for the visitors to be seated in order to be entertained by a team of dancers, Miss Milligan, directed by the Duke, assumed the chair intended for the principal guest; consequently, she viewed the dancing from the "throne" with the Queen on her right and the royal consort seated on a stool on her left. Undoubtedly, the royal visit was one of the highlights of Miss Milligan's life; the Duke's teasing and the Queen's knowledge of

Miss Milligan, Miss Hadden and Lady Elgin with the Queen and the Duke of Edinburgh during the royal visit to RSCDS Headquarters, 28th June 1961.

country dancing were frequently recalled in the many accounts she gave of that important day.

Along with such significant developments for the Society during the years 1950 to 1970, Miss Milligan had her own personal achievements. In 1951 she directed her attention once more to authorship. Miss Milligan's dexterity with words, both written and spoken, is well known. No doubt this skill was largely the result of a literary education begun early in life under her mother's tutelage. Although in adulthood she enjoyed a good detective story, love of the classic works of English and Scottish literature remained with her all her life and enabled her to quote liberally and aptly from them. For example, classes of advanced dancers would hear Chaucer's words, "If gold rust, what shall iron do?", when their poor efforts displeased their teacher. The book with which Miss Milligan was probably most familiar was her Bible, from which she was never long parted, and Biblical texts were used both to encourage and reprimand classes. Scots words and phrases, with which she had been familiar since childhood, were introduced into lessons, much to the bewilderment of many who heard them. "What does that mean?", she would ask and, half jokingly, would scold the Scots present for a disappointing ignorance of native idiom.

Miss Milligan's first venture into print, *The Festival Booklet*, has already been mentioned. Her next book, *Won't You Join the Dance* was issued by Paterson's Publications in 1951 and became the official manual of the Society. Her very popular *101 Scottish Country Dances* and *99 More Country Dances* appeared in 1956 and 1963 respectively and in the same series, published by Collins, Miss Milligan provided a very helpful guide to Scottish country dancing in her book *Introducing Scottish Country Dancing*.

A new activity to which Miss Milligan turned her attention in 1950, was film making. The Scottish Educational Film Association and the Scottish Film Council, with the co-operation of the Scottish Country Dance Society, produced, as aids to teaching, a series of films and short loop films on Scottish country dancing. Miss Milligan acted as Dance Supervisor. Six years later, when the RSCDS collaborated with Films of Scotland in producing "Scotland Dances", the dancing sequences, in settings ranging from the elegant Edinburgh Assembly Rooms to an Ayrshire cornfield, were also supervised by her. A contemporary record describes Miss Milligan in action:

> She stood among drying stooks in a cornfield near Ayr, guiding a team of local dancers. Dressed in 18th century costume, they danced "Corn Riggs" for two hours. The field was soggy. Stubble scratched the dancers' feet. Beside the camera, Miss Milligan urged them on: "Be gay. You're supposed to be happy. Keep it up. Put more life into it," she called.[25]

She had the opportunity to appear on the screen herself in 1972 when the RSCDS was asked by the BBC to participate in a film entitled "Mr. Menuhin's Welcome to Blair Castle". This was a delightful documentary about Scotland's traditional fiddle music. Miss Milligan is seen and heard in conversation with Yehudi Menuhin; the meeting was obviously enjoyed by both.

"DANCE WITH YOUR SOUL"
Miss Milligan directing a sequence for "Scotland Dances" in 1956.

Filming, writing, teaching, examining, attending committee meetings and travelling abroad – there was no lessening of Miss Milligan's many activities despite advancing years and the onset of painful arthritis. At times the work must have been very exacting for an octogenarian but, in all that she did, Miss Milligan continued to find great pleasure and satisfaction. After the Summer School of 1968, she confided to a correspondent, "Though very tired when I was at last off the chain!! I had a grand feeling of satisfaction." Miss Milligan's undiminished enthusiasm, her indomitable spirit and amazing physical stamina astonished everybody. The idea of giving up, if ever contemplated, was instantly dismissed; quoting H. W. Longfellow, she used to say, "My departure will be like the Arabs who fold their tents and silently steal away." Once into the decade of the 70s, there was a great incentive to keep going because the Society was now approaching its fiftieth anniversary. The Jubilee of 1973 proved to be an outstanding occasion in the life of the Royal Scottish Country Dance Society and of its co-founder.

References

1. *SCDS Bulletin*, No. 27, October 1949, p. 12.
2. *Ibid.*, p. 3.
3. *SCDS Bulletin*, No. 29, October 1951, p. 1.
4. *RSCDS Bulletin*, No. 47, October 1969, p. 19.
5. *RSCDS Bulletin*, No. 35, October 1957, p. 28.
6. *RSCDS Bulletin*, No. 31, October 1953, p. 25.
7. SCDS, Minutes of Meetings of the Executive Council, 6 Aug. & 30 Oct. 1948.
8. *Ibid.*, 5 Dec. 1959.
9. *SCDS Bulletin*, No. 29, October 1951, p. 25.
10. *RSCDS Bulletin*, No. 33, October 1955, 28.
11. RSCDS Boston Branch, *Tartan Times Special Issue 1923–1973*, p. 14; RSCDS Toronto Branch, *Silver Jubilee Book 1957–1982*, p. 8.
12. Alan & Lydia Smith, "She's O.K.", *Tartan Times Special Issue 1923–1973*, p. 17.
13. *RSCDS Bulletin*, No. 36, October 1958, p. 1.
14. *RSCDS Bulletin*, No. 55, October 1977, p. 7.
15. *RSCDS Bulletin*, No. 53, October 1975, p. 23.
16. RSCDS Log, Vol. 2.
17. A Pictorial Record of Miss Milligan's Visit to New Zealand in 1974.
18. RSCDS, Minutes of Meetings of the Executive Council, 18 May 1957; *RSCDS Bulletin*, No. 40, October 1962, p. 31.
19. *SCDS Bulletin*, No. 22, December 1944, p. 1.
20. SCDS Bulletin, No. 24, October 1946, p. 1.
21. *RSCDS Bulletin*, No. 31, October 1953, p. 1.
22. *RSCDS Bulletin*, No. 33, October 1955, p. 1.
23. *RSCDS Bulletin*, No. 45, October 1967, p. 2.
24. *RSCDS Bulletin*, No. 39, October 1961, p. 1.
25. RSCDS Log, Vol. 1.

8 The Jubilee

During 1973, the year of the eagerly awaited Golden Jubilee of the Royal Scottish Country Dance Society, Miss Milligan was the recipient of many tributes. In the month of June it was announced by the *Evening Times* that its readers had voted her "Scotswoman of the Year". This is an annual event organised by the Glasgow newspaper which invites from its readers nominations for the title and, subsequently, for votes on the nominees. Society members rallied round their leader, canvassing their non-dancing friends so enthusiastically that Miss Milligan was assured of victory over fourteen other candidates. The *Evening Times* declared, "This 'First Lady of the Dance' is a most successful ambassadress for Scotland . . . inspiring thousands of people in all quarters of the globe with a love and enthusiasm for the dance."[1]

The Lady Provost of Glasgow, Mrs. William Gray, presenting Miss Milligan, Scotswoman of the Year, with the *Evening Times* silver rosebowl, 19th June 1973. (*Picture by courtesy of the* Evening Times)

At a special luncheon, the principal guest was the "Scotswoman of the Year" for 1973. Among the 200 other guests, who represented the major women's organisations of Scotland, were Miss Molly Weir, the Glasgow writer and actress, and Mrs. Margaret Parker, presently Chairman of the Royal Scottish Country Dance Society. When presented with the *Evening Times* silver rosebowl by Mrs. William Gray, Lady Provost of Glasgow, Miss Milligan in reply said, "I very humbly receive this lovely bowl because I am only the representative of the society which I think is the most wonderful in the world."[2]

The year of the Golden Jubilee was both a memorable and a busy one for Miss Milligan. The celebrations began in April with a Jubilee Reunion Dinner held by Glasgow, the Society's first and oldest Branch, which considered itself very fortunate in 1973 that its President was the co-founder and that another founder member, Miss Lilian Ross, was its Chairman. Other branches followed with their own festivities and Miss Milligan's presence was requested at most if not all of them. As she herself said, "So much is happening this year, I am on a non-stop round of attending birthday parties and cutting cakes."[3] Throughout the year a continual stream of invitations and congratulations poured into her home in Saltoun Street, Glasgow. Miss Milligan always enjoyed receiving letters from her country dance family and, being a conscientious correspondent, endeavoured to reply to each one in her own hand. At times this was a difficult task. She once remarked, "I have just posted about 14 (letters) today but it still looks as if a mouse had nibbled at the pile."[4] The flood of correspondence in 1973 proved too much, even for the energetic and willing lady, and the following notice had to be inserted in the *RSCDS Bulletin*:

> Miss J. C. Milligan wishes to thank all those who kindly wrote most welcome letters which she greatly enjoys reading but begs them to forgive her for not replying as she finds it impossible to write personally to everyone.[5]

In addition to her interest in and attendance at functions organised by the individual branches, Miss Milligan, of course, also took a leading part in arrangements for the Society's own commemoration of the Fiftieth Anniversary. As early as 4th December 1971, she spoke to the Executive Council about the approaching Jubilee and emphasised that, although events were planned for Glasgow and St. Andrews, this was to be a celebration for the whole Society because she had "toiled since the formation to instil a family feeling into members." A souvenir brochure would provide a record of events for those not able to attend.[6] "1973 must be celebrated in such a way that it becomes a never-to-be-forgotten year, treasured for ever in the archives of the Society," she wrote in the *Bulletin* of 1972.[7]

The "official" RSCDS celebrations began in splendour on

Miss Milligan receiving a presentation goblet from Mr. D. McLean at the Jubilee Reunion Dinner of the Glasgow Branch held in the Albany Hotel on Friday, 6th April 1973.

Thursday, 12th July with a Jubilee Ball in the Assembly Rooms, Edinburgh, attended by the royal patron of the Society, Queen Elizabeth, with the Duke of Edinburgh and Princess Anne. The Queen delighted not only Miss Milligan but all members by the genuine interest she showed on this occasion. As she intended to bring several of her house guests to the Ball from Holyrood, where she was in residence, she asked for a copy of the programme beforehand,

Miss Milligan joining in the combined Jubilee celebrations of the Castle Douglas, Gatehouse and Kirkcudbright Branches. From left to right: Mr. W. Little, Miss Milligan, Mrs. W. Wadsworth, Mrs. L. Brown, Mr. A. McCulloch, Mrs. W. McKell.

Lord Macdonald (RSCDS President) presenting to the Queen and the Duke of Edinburgh Miss Milligan, Mr. J. B. C. Brown (RSCDS Chairman), Mrs. Brown and Miss Florence H. Adams (RSCDS Vice-Chairman) at the Jubilee Ball, Edinburgh, 12 July 1973. (*Picture by courtesy of The Scotsman*)

The Royal Patron dancing with Sir Ian Moncrieffe of that Ilk at the Jubilee Ball in the Assembly Rooms, Edinburgh, Thursday, 12th July 1973. (*Picture by courtesy of the Daily Record*)

suggested some dances she would like included and taught some – with varying success! – to the houseparty. The Queen herself, having been taught Scottish dances as a child, is an expert and graceful dancer. The compliment to the Society most apreciated by Miss Milligan was that Her Majesty dressed for the occasion, not in regal attire, but in the simple and suitable clothing worn by the other ladies at the Ball. Henceforward a photograph of Queen Elizabeth leading off the dance with Sir Ian Moncrieffe of that Ilk took pride of place on Miss Milligan's mantelpiece in her Glasgow flat.

During the 1973 Summer School the Town and University of St. Andrews honoured the RSCDS by arranging various Jubilee functions. These included a Civic Reception, dinners given by the University Court and by Miss Lorna Walker of University Hall, the principal residence of the Summer School, and several enjoyable dances in the Younger Hall. The event which will linger longest in the memory is the St. Andrews Garden Party, because it provided a wonderful opportunity for members, apart from Officebearers and the Executive Council, to have a chat with the legendary Miss Milligan. The Garden Party, the brainchild of the Chairman, Mr. James B. Brown, was open to all and from far and near they came in their hundreds, many bringing their children to share in the family gathering. All afternoon, with her fur cape over her arm, for after an unpromising morning, the sun came out in brilliance, the indefatigable lady chatted to eager groups of men, women and children. Sometimes in serious mood, more often laughing over amusing reminiscences, she was never less than her buoyant self. Like her "posse" of sandwich makers, who managed to feed the hundreds twice during the party, she must have been completely exhausted when the sun went in and the last guests reluctantly departed. No one present that day will ever forget the unique occasion when Miss Milligan met so many of her family.

The most formal event of 1973 was the Annual General Meeting of the Society in November which fittingly took place in its birthplace, Glasgow. Miss Milligan had planned well ahead to make sure that the pervading spirit of the Golden Jubilee should be friendship. In pursuance of this aim, she laid down the law, with customary firmness: "Only the minimum of necessary business to be included in the agenda. No new resolutions nor amendments, however seemingly straight forward, to be accepted." So the meeting passed smoothly and swiftly. Miss Milligan's own contribution to the social aspect of the Weekend might have daunted a much younger woman. So great had been the number of applications for the Friday evening Ball that Glasgow Branch had been obliged to arrange late night dances in four different venues. After attending a Civic Reception in the City Chambers, Miss Milligan was ferried to each of them in turn, to be

Miss Milligan at the Jubilee
Garden Party, St. Andrews, 15th
August 1973.

Surveying another contribution
to her "Mile of Pennies",
St. Andrews, August 1973.

Arriving at the City Chambers,
Glasgow, for the Jubilee Civic
Reception, 2nd November 1973.

greeted, not surprisingly, at the last, the Albany Hotel, with a standing ovation and the unanimous singing of "For She's a Jolly Good Fellow".[8]

The Jubilee Lunch before the AGM developed the theme of friendship in two official and, of course, many personal ways. Miss Milligan's "Mile of Pennies", which reached the astounding sum of £1,800, ensured that every member who wished to attend was present and, after the usual toasts, came another of her innovations. In the *Jubilee Brochure* this is described very vividly:

> Short messages of greeting and congratulation were then delivered by representatives of fourteen countries furth of Scotland. From Australia, Belgium and Canada they came: from England and from France; from Germany, whose representative, tongue-tied by a foreign language, could only smile and give a dignified bow, but his meaning was clear; from Holland and Northern Ireland, the latter touchingly describing how the weekly dancing class was a haven of peace and friendship and happiness in a beleaguered Belfast; from far-off New Zealand and South Africa; from Switzerland, Eastern U.S.A. and Western U.S.A., and, finally, from our fellow Celts in Wales.[9]

The AGM Weekend of 1973 concluded on Saturday evening with an informal dance at Jordanhill College of Education. This was a very appropriate venue for the last event because, in the words of the *Jubilee Brochure*, "If any particular location in Glasgow can be considered to be the womb of the Society, that place is Jordanhill College, for Miss Milligan was a teacher there in 1923 and many members of the College staff and even more of the students have been (and still are) active and important members of the Society." The *Brochure* continues:

> Thus ended a wonderful weekend, the culmination of fifty years of the Society's existence. But it was more than that, for it was the opening page of the history of the second half-century of the R.S.C.D.S.[10]

With the commencement of a new chapter in its history, Miss Milligan showed no signs of reducing her considerable commitment to the affairs of the Society to which she had already given so much during the previous fifty years. As Vice-President, and as caretaker President for the year 1976–7, her presence was required at all committee meetings. Examining and teaching tours at home and abroad continued as before, material for the Society's next book of traditional dances had to be found and arrangements made for the Summer Schools at St. Andrews. To the delight of all members, this tireless dedication to the work of the Society at last received formal recognition, in July 1977, when the University of Aberdeen conferred the honorary degree of Doctor of Laws upon the co-founder. Professor Fraser who, in his presentation of Miss Milligan at the degree ceremony, described her as "a quite remarkable woman", concluded his laureation thus:

> Dancing and the music which accompanies it is very much part of our national heritage. Miss Milligan is directly responsible for the healthy state of the first, and indirectly for the astounding revival of interest in the second – after all, Yehudi Menuhin himself has become one of its devotees. It is right that this University should recognise her contribution and pay tribute to her as an individual.[11]

The Royal Scottish Country Dance Society wholeheartedly applauded this tribute and was deeply grateful to the University of Aberdeen for so honouring the lady who had helped to create it and under whose inspiring leadership it had flourished for so long.

Jean Callander Milligan, LL.D., July 1977.

References

1. *Evening Times* (Glasgow), June 15, 1973, p. 6.
2. *Ibid.*, June 20, 1973, p. 6.
3. *Ibid.*, June 15, 1973, p. 6.
4. Doreen Taylor, "At home with Jean Milligan", *Scottish Field* (August, 1975), pp. 56–7.
5. *RSCDS Bulletin*, No. 51 (October, 1973), p. 2.
6. RSCDS, Minutes of Meetings of the Executive Council, Dec. 4, 1971.
7. *RSCDS Bulletin*, No. 50 (October, 1972), p. 2.
8. *RSCDS Golden Jubilee 1923–1973* (Jubilee Brochure).
9. *Ibid.*
10. *Ibid.*
11. *Aberdeen University Review*, Vol. XLVII, No. 159 (Spring, 1978), pp. 277–9.

With the staff and students of the
July course of the Summer
School.

Being piped into a Summer
School ceilidh.

Conclusion

On 28th July 1978, the news of Dr. Milligan's sudden death was announced. Tributes poured in from all over the world, but probably the words of friends and colleagues in Scotland most fittingly round off this memoir of her long, unique life.

In August, a Memorial Service, held in St. Leonard's Parish Church, St. Andrews, was conducted by the late Reverend Andrew McLellan who, for many years, acted as honorary chaplain to the RSCDS Summer School. In his address Mr. McLellan commented on Dr. Milligan's conviction that "dancing should come from the heart" and said:

> I am sure that that explains just about everything about Dr. Milligan. Through those long years it was that great heart of hers which so often gave heart to Scottish Country Dancing, to the dancing itself and to the movement for popularising it.

When Glasgow paid tribute in the following November, Miss Isobel Elliot, then Branch Chairman, reminded those present of Dr. Milligan's deep-rooted interest in music, teaching, her native country, Scotland, and, above all, its dances. A former colleague and Principal of Jordanhill College, Sir Henry Wood, recalling his first attempt at Scottish country dancing and the lecture from Miss Milligan it had provoked, acknowledged that she could be "impetuous and imperious at times." Sir Henry concluded his remarks by saying that he would remember Dr. Milligan "as a great teacher who thoroughly enjoyed teaching and who was not afraid to tell the world that she was a teacher and that she loved it." The last words of tribute came from Mr. Duncan Macleod, Chairman of the Royal Scottish Country Dance Society in 1978. As one of "her boys" who had been in close touch with her for many years, Mr. Macleod said about Dr. Milligan:

> As one came to know her better one realised that she was a woman of great simplicities and great complexities. An inspiration to many, a comfort to others. A woman who possessed great courage, tremendous determination and drive, remarkable zest, an outstanding teacher and leader, and with all of this full of fun and joy.

Dr. Milligan will live in the memory of her friends as one who enjoyed life to the full. In one of her last letters to a College student of 1917–19, she described Christmas 1977: "My old assistant and great friend Margaret McLaren came to stay with me. We hung up each other's stockings and had great fun." With equal enjoyment she celebrated her ninety-second birthday barely three weeks before her death. Even when faced by the unavoidable ills of life, Dr. Milligan managed to conceal the pain with an enviable appearance of gaiety.

In the words of the great dancer, Anna Pavlova, Dr. Milligan could well have said, "I desire that my message of beauty and joy and life shall be taken up after me." To thousands of dancers, musicians and teachers throughout the world, the Royal Scottish Country Dance Society is her legacy of friendship and fun. Only by striving, with her spirit, to maintain the standards she set, can her family of Scottish country dancers show to the world their appreciation of that very distinguished Scotswoman, Dr. Jean Callander Milligan.

Sources Consulted

PRIMARY SOURCES Addresses given were the locations of sources at the time of consultation.

Government Records

1. General Register Office, Princes Street, Edinburgh.
   Census Returns (Hillhead, Roxburgh, Denny), 1841, 1851, 1861, 1871, 1881, 1891.
   Registers of Births, Marriages and Deaths (Scotland).
2. General Register Office, St. Catherine's House, Kingsway, London.
   Census Returns (St. Pancras, London), 1871.
   Register of Marriages (Marylebone, London), 1876.

Church Records

1. HM General Register House, Princes Street, Edinburgh.
   Records of Births, Marriages and Deaths for the Parishes of Denny, Falkirk and Roxburgh (before 1841).
   Session Records of Finnieston Free Church, Glasgow, 1861–1869.
2. United Reformed Church House, Tavistock Place, London.
   Session Records of Regent Square and St. John's Wood English Presbyterian Churches, London, 1870–1876.
3. Wellington Church, University Avenue, Hillhead, Glasgow.
   Session Records of Wellington Street United Presbyterian Church, Glasgow, 1862–1873.
   Reports of the Religious Institutions in Connection with Wellington Street Congregation, Glasgow, 1863–1873.

University and College Records

1. University of Glasgow, Hillhead, Glasgow.
   Registers of Members of the General Council of the University of Glasgow, 1876–1913.
   Annual Reports of the Queen Margaret College Settlement Association, 1928–1932.
2. Jordanhill College of Education, Southbrae Drive, Glasgow.
   Register of Students Attending the Glasgow Established Church Training College During Session 1864, 1865 and 1866.
   Register of Students, Free Training College, 1845–1881.
   Glasgow Provincial Committe for the Training of Teachers, Minutes of Meetings, 1905–1948.
   The Training College Magazine, 1907–1914, 1923.
   The New Dominie, 1927–1948.
3. Dartford Faculty of Education and Movement Studies (Thames Polytechnic), Oakfield Lane, Dartford.
   Registers of Gymnastic Teachers and Medical Gymnasts Trained at Madame Bergman-Österberg's Physical Training College, 1885–1908, 1913, 1922.
   Madame Österberg's Physical Training College Reports, 1895, 1896–1898.
   Magazine of the Bergman-Österberg Union of Trained Gymnastic (or *The Bergman-Österberg Physical Training College Magazine*), 1917–1935.

School Records

1. Glasgow Room, Mitchell Library, North Street, Glasgow.
   Prospectuses of the Glasgow High School for Girls, 1901–1914.

The Glasgow Academy Chronicle, 1899–1926.
2. Strathclyde Regional Archives, City Chambers, Glasgow.
   Garnethill Public School (Glasgow High School for Girls), Headmaster's Letter Books, 1892, 1895, 1905.
   Admission Register, Garnethill Public School, 1885–1899.
   Log Book, Glasgow High School for Girls.
3. Glasgow Academy, Colebrooke Street, Glasgow.
   Glasgow Academy Rolls, 1890–1900.

National and International Organisations

1. The Royal Scottish Country Dance Society, 12 Coates Crescent, Edinburgh.
   Minutes of Meetings of the following:
       Interim Executive Committee, 1923–1924.
       Annual General Meetings, 1924–1932.
       Executive Council, 1924–1978.
       Publications Committee, 1934–1978.
       Management Committee, 1942–1952.
       Fife Branch, 1929–1937.
       Perth and Perthshire Branch, 1932–1956.
       Duns and District Branch, 1953–1959.
   SCDS Secretary's Examination Book, 1924–1937.
   Dr. Jean C. Milligan's Notebooks.
   SCDS (RSCDS) Bulletins, 1932–1979 (these contain the Annual Reports which prior to 1932 are available in the Minutes of the Executive Council).
   RSCDS Log, 2 Vols. (an historical record in photographs, newspaper cuttings etc.).
   A Pictorial Record of Miss Milligan's Visit to New Zealand in 1974.
   Also made available for consultation were the following:
       Manchester Branch, Minutes of Meetings, 1935–1949.
       Rochdale Branch, A Record of its History.
2. Glasgow Keep Fit Movement, Royal Crescent, Glasgow.
   GKFM, Minutes of Meetings, 1934–1941.
3. The British Red Cross, Grosvenor Crescent, London.
   Jean C. Milligan's Record Card, 1915–1916.
4. The Ling Association (now The Physical Education Association), Ling House, Nottingham Place, London.
   Ling Association, Minutes of Meetings of the Executive Committee, 1921–1931.
   The Ling Association Annual Reports, 1919–1943.
   The Monthly Leaflet of the Ling Association, 1908–1948.
   Journal of School Hygiene and Physical Education (from 1933 *Journal of Physical Education and School Hygiene*), 1922–1943.

Newspapers

1. Mitchell Library, Glasgow.
   Glasgow Herald, 1886, 1910, 1912, 1923, 1978.
   Evening Times (Glasgow), 1973.
2. Motherwell Public Library, Hamilton Road, Motherwell.
   Motherwell Times, 1932–1937.

SECONDARY SOURCES

A Roll of the Graduates of the University of Glasgow 1727–1897, compiled by W. Innes Addison (Glasgow: Maclehose, 1898).
Brown, May, *Alive In The 1900s* (Edinburgh: The Scottish Sports Council, 1979).

Cruickshank, Marjorie, *History of the Training of Teachers in Scotland* (London: University of London Press, 1970).

Glasgow in Panorama (Glasgow: Glasgow Herald, 1906).

Fairley, J. A., *Jordanhill College of Education 1921–1971* (Glasgow, 1974).

Fonteyn, Margot, *The Magic of Dance* (London: BBC, 1980)

Henderson, I. A. N., "Jean Milligan: The First Lady of the Dance", *The Scots Magazine*, Jan., 1973, pp. 365–371.

Hillhead High School Magazine, Vol. XVI (Dec., 1929), Vol. XXXIV (Dec., 1948).

Historical Pageant. The Story of the West (Glasgow, 1928).

Holtby, Winifred, *Letters to a Friend*, edited by Alice Holtby & Jean McWilliam (London: Collins, 1937).

Jordanhill College School Magazine, 1941, 1945.

MacLean, Isabella C., *The History of Dunfermline College of Physical Education* (Edinburgh, 1976).

May, J., *Madame Bergman-Österberg* (London: University of London Institute of Education, 1969).

Milligan, Jean C., *Won't You Join the Dance* (London: Paterson's Publications, 1982 Revised Edition).

Milligan, Jean C., *The Scottish Country Dance, Festival Booklets*, edited by F. H. Bisset (Glasgow & London: Paterson's Publications, 1924).

Milligan, Jean C. & MacLennan, D. G., *Dances of Scotland* (London: Max Parrish & Co. Ltd., 1950).

Milligan, Jean C., *Introducing Scottish Country Dancing* (Glasgow & London: Collins, 1968).

101 Scottish Country Dances, compiled by Jean C. Milligan (Glasgow & London: Collins, 1956).

99 More Scottish Country Dances, compiled by Jean C. Milligan (Glasgow & London: Collins, 1963).

Milligan, Isabel M., "1891–1898", *Girls' High School Magazine*, No. 29 (June, 1944, Jubilee Number), pp. 7–12.

Reports by the Joint War Committee of the Joint War Finance Committee of the British Red Cross Society and the Order of St. John of Jerusalem in England 1914–1919 (London: HMSO, 1921).

Roxburgh, J. M., *The School Board of Glasgow* (London: University of London Press, 1971).

RSCDS Golden Jubilee 1923–1973 (Jubilee Brochure, 1973).

RSCDS Toronto Branch Silver Jubilee 1957–1982 (Toronto, 1982).

Smallwood, Mirth, "Miss Milligan in New Zealand", *New Zealand Scottish Country Dancer*, Vol. 22 (1975), pp. 19–20.

Smith, Alan & Lydia, "She's O.K.!", *Tartan Times. Special Issue. 1923–1973*, pp. 17–18.

Stevenson, A. L., "The Development of Physical Education in the State Schools of Scotland 1900–1960" (unpublished M.Litt. dissertation, University of Aberdeen, 1978).

Taylor, Doreen, "At home with Jean Milligan", *Scottish Field*, Aug., 1975, pp. 56–57.

The Scottish School of Physical Education. A Jubilee Souvenir Chronicle. Chronicled by David Wilson, O.B.E., F.E.I.S. (Glasgow, 1981).

University of Aberdeen Review, Vol. XXVII, No. 159, Spring, 1978.

Index